The People of
GLASGOW
and
CLYDESDALE
at Home and Abroad
1800-1850

By
David Dobson

Copyright © 2022
by David Dobson
All Rights Reserved

Published for Clearfield Company by
Genealogical Publishing Company
Baltimore, Maryland
2022

ISBN: 9780806359489

INTRODUCTION TO PEOPLE OF GLASGOW AND CLYDESDALE AT HOME AND ABROAD, 1800-1850

This book identifies people resident in Glasgow and in neighbouring Clydesdale (alias Lanarkshire), as well as persons abroad who originated in these locations, during the first half of the 19th century. By 1800, the economy of Glasgow, which had become highly dependent on transatlantic trade, had begun to industrialise. The colonial British Navigation Acts and various geo-political factors had given Glasgow a major advantage in trade with the Thirteen Colonies of North America. (This favoured relationship ended with American Independence, which had a significant impact on the tobacco trade between the Chesapeake and the Clyde.) The profits from the tobacco, sugar, cotton, and timber trades, furthermore, enabled entrepreneurs in and around Glasgow to diversify their investments. Capital increasingly was invested in collieries and iron mines, engineering, shipbuilding, and textile factories to produce goods for export. The burgeoning population of Glasgow also caused an expansion of agriculture along the Clyde Valley. In 1800 the city of Glasgow had nearly 80,000 inhabitants, and by 1850 it had increased to around 330,00 people. Part of this increase stemmed from immigration from the West Highlands and from Ireland. By mid-century, Glasgow had become the 'Second City of Empire'.

Glasgow's rapid growth was not without its growing pains. Its expanding population, however, gave rise to grave social problems, including the exploitation of the working class, child labour, and poor wages. Typhus and cholera also contributed to the urban crisis. The trade cycle, especially in the aftermath of the Napoleonic Wars in 1815, caused social unrest and rioting, known as the 'Radical War'. The most prominent groups amongst the rioters were the colliers and the weavers; many of the latter chose to emigrate to North America including an immigrant ancestor of Ronald Reagan. Glasgow also developed commercial services such as banking and insurance, that facilitated economic growth. This skilled, white-collar work force was in demand abroad, especially in the rapidly industrializing United States. This too contributed to emigration.

The Clyde Valley, alias upper Clydesdale, was basically agricultural, and contained several small burghs, such as Lanark. A notable development in the neighbourhood of Lanark was a model industrial village named New Lanark. It was established by the philanthropist David Dale in 1783 as a cotton spinning centre. By 1792, its workforce reached 1,157, of whom 800 were children. The project was under the management of Robert Owen from 1825. It was an experiment in housing, factory management, and education. Owen provided workers with shorter hours, free health care, and education. He also attempted to reproduce his ideas in New Harmony, Indiana. New Lanark is now a World Heritage Site.

For those genealogists with their roots in or around Glasgow there are two Family History Societies, one is the Glasgow and West of Scotland FHS, at 32 Mansfield Street, Glasgow; and the other is the Lanarkshire FHS, High Road, Motherwell. The best single genealogy library in the area is the Mitchell Library, North Street, Glasgow, which claims to be one of the largest reference libraries in Europe.

David Dobson,
Dundee, Scotland, 2022

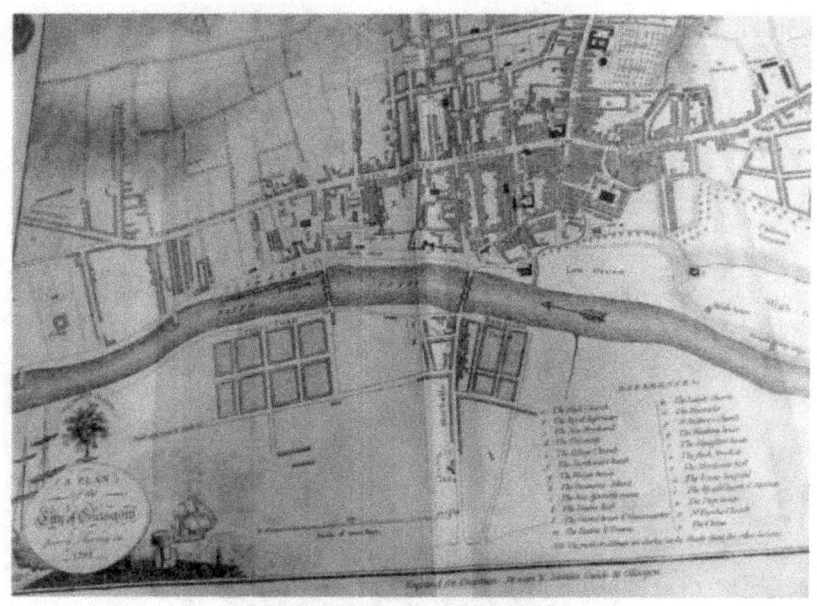

Street map of Glasgow, 1797

Trongate, Glasgow

Glasgow and Clyde river

Glasgow landscape

View of the Merchants House, Bridgegate, Glasgow

The Royal Exchange, formerly the residence of
William Cunninghame, tobacco merchant

View of the Barracks, Glasgow

View of Saint Enoch's Church, the Surgeons Hall, and Square

The Gallowgate, Glasgow

Buchanan Street, Glasgow

PEOPLE OF GLASGOW AND CLYDESDALE

AT HOME AND ABROAD, 1800-1850

ADAM, DAVID, of the Brownfield and Anderston Emigration Society, emigrated via Greenock on board the Earl of Buckinghamshire, Captain Johnston, bound for Quebec on 29 April 1821, was granted land in Ramsay, Upper Canada, on 26 July 1821. [TNA.CO42.189] [PAO]

ADAMS, GILBERT, born in Louisville, Kentucky, graduated MD Glasgow University in 1853. [RGG]

ADAM, HENRY, an engineer in Mexico, heir to his grandmother Mary Robertson, wife of John Galt a mason in Govan, who died on 23 November 1859. [NRS.S/H]

ADAM, JAMES, in Cambridge, USA, heir to his grandmother Mary Robertson, wife of John Galt a mason in Govan, who died on 23 November 1859. [NRS.S/H]

ADAMS, ….., from Glasgow, aboard the Betsy and Brothers bound for Jamaica, landed in Kingston in May 1793. [JRG.25.5.1794]

AFFLECK, JAMES, born 1782 in Lanarkshire, a sawyer, was accused of discharging a firearm and wounding in Penicuik, Midlothian, in1832. [NRS.AD14.32.384]

AIKEN, JAMES, a carrier in Glasgow, note books, 1805-1806. [NRS.CS96.4337]

AIKEN, ROBERT, a baker, was admitted as a burgess and guilds-brother of Glasgow on 6 February 1818, having served his apprenticeship under John Ronald a baker, burgess and guilds-brother. [GBR]

AIR, ANDREW, a founder in Glasgow, married Ann Smith on 7 December 1834. [Glasgow OPR]

AIRD, JOHN, born 1821, from Strathaven, emigrated via Greenock aboard the William Rodger, master John Reid, landed in New South Wales on 26 September 1838. [NSWpa]

AITKEN, DAVID, born 1827 in Carnwath, son of William Aitken, a smith, and his wife Margaret Anderson, died in Goodwell, Jamaica on 8 March 1847. [Carnwath gravestone]

AITKEN, JOHN, born in Cumbernauld in 1806, a merchant in New York, died there on 6 January 1879. [ANY]

AITKENHEAD, JAMES, President of the Strathaven and Kilbride Emigration Society, with his wife and family, emigrated via Greenock aboard the George Canning, Captain Potter, bound for Quebec on 14 April 1821. [TNA.CO42.189]

AITON, WILLIAM, from Strathaven, applied to settle in Canada on 27 February 1815. [NRS.RH9]

ALCORN, SIMON, of the Spring Bank Emigration Society, and family, emigrated via Greenock aboard the Commerce of Greenock, Captain Covendale, bound for Quebec on 11 May 1821. [TNA.CO42.189]

ALEXANDER, HUGH, born 1777, eldest son of John Alexander a merchant in Glasgow, died at Eden Hill, St Mary's, Jamaica, in 1802. [AJ.2867][GkAd.100]

ALEXANDER, JANE, born 1789 in Lanarkshire, emigrated via Glasgow on board the Lady Campbell, bound for St John, New Brunswick in 1834. [PANB.RS23]

ALEXANDER, JOHN, born 1813 in Lanarkshire, emigrated via Glasgow on board the Lady Campbell, bound for St John, New Brunswick in 1833. [PANB.RS23]

ALEXANDER, Mrs SARAH, born 1797, died in Auckland, New Zealand, in February 1864. [Lanark gravestone]

ALLAN, or BLACK, GEORGE, a burglar, was sentenced to be transported to the colonies for 14 years, at Glasgow on 26 April 1811. [SM.83.5/393]

ALLAN, JAMES, of the Glasgow Wrights Emigration Society, emigrated via Greenock aboard the George Canning, Captain Potter, bound for Quebec on 14 April 1821. [TNA.CO42.189]

ALLAN, ROBERT, born 1810, a gardener from the Gorbals, Glasgow, emigrated via Greenock aboard the William Rodger, master John Reid, landed in New South Wales on 26 September 1838. [NSWpa]

ALLAN, ROBERT, master of the Montreal of Glasgow from Greenock to Quebec and Montreal in 1814. [NRS.E504.15.104]

ALLAN, WILLIAM, a weaver from Glasgow, settled in Dalhousie township, Upper Canada, around 1821. [BPP.2.167]

ALLAN, Captain, master of the Favourite of Port Glasgow from the River Clyde with passengers to Montreal and Quebec in 1830, 1831, 1832, 1833. [GA]; master of the Glencairn of Glasgow with passengers bound for Quebec in 1851. [SRA.T/CN.26/5]

ALLASON, DAVID, son of Zachariah Allason and his wife Isabel Hall in Gorbals, an indentured servant bound for Rappahannock, Virginia in 1757, in Falmouth, Va., from 1760 to 1762, a storekeeper in Winchester, Va., in 1763, died after 1815. [SRA][VMHB.1931]

ALLAN, WILLIAM, a merchant from Glasgow, was naturalised in South Carolina on 16 January 1798. [NARA.M1183.1]

ALSTON, JAMES W., married Marion Cross, youngest daughter of William Cross, in Glasgow, on 8 October 1822. [SM.90.631]

ANDERSON, HUGH, from Glasgow, was naturalised in South Carolina on 11 May 1821. [NARA.M1183.1]

ANDERSON, HUGH, of the Barrowfield Road Emigration Society, emigrated via Greenock aboard the George Canning, Captain Potter, bound for Quebec on 14 April 1821. [TNA.CO42.189]

ANDERSON, JAMES, born 20 June 1785, son of William Anderson and his wife Elizabeth Bell, graduated MA from Edinburgh University in 1813, minister at Blantyre from 1832 until his death on 7 May 1860. [F.3.229]

ANDERSON, JOHN, born 1775, formerly of the 23rd Light Dragoons later a weaver in Anderston, Barony parish, Glasgow, with his wife Grace born 1778, and children Isabella born 1801, Elizabeth born 1806,

Thomas born 1809, John born 1812, James born 1814, Ann born 1816, and Samuel born 1819, applied to emigrate to Canada on 30 September 1820. [TNA.CO384.6.73]

ANDERSON, JOHN, a writer in Glasgow, son of Thomas Anderson a merchant in Glasgow, was admitted as a Notary Public on 22 December 1791, died 8 May 1826. [NRS.NP2.34.313]

ANDERSON, JOHN, a manufacturer in Lanark, dead before 1826, father of Stephen Anderson a surgeon in Pisco, South America. [NRS.S/H]

ANDERSON, JOHN, a manufacturer in Lanark, father of Stephen Anderson, a surgeon in Pisco, Peru, 1826. [NRS.S/H]

ANDERSON, WILLIAM, of the Rutherglen Emigration Society, with his wife, three sons, and three daughters, emigrated via Greenock aboard the Commerce of Greenock, Captain Covendale, bound for Quebec on 11 May 1821, was granted land in Ramsay, Upper Canada, on 9 September 1821. [TNA.CO42.189][PAO]

ANDERSON, ..., agent in Lanark for the Western Bank of Scotland in 1849. [POD]

ANDREW, JOHN, formerly a reaper, later a weaver in Lanark, was accused of bigamy in 1822. [NRS.AD14.22.167]

ANDREW, ROBERT, born 1799, a malt dealer in Rutherglen Loan, Gorbals, was accused of cattle stealing in 1836. [NRS.AD14.36.288]

ANGUS, ANDREW, of the Rutherglen Emigration Society, emigrated via Greenock aboard the Commerce of Greenock, Captain Covendale, bound for Quebec on 11 May 1821, was granted land in Lanark, Upper Canada, on 4 September 1821. [TNA.CO42.189][PAO]

ANGUS, JOHN, of the Rutherglen Emigration Society, with his wife, son and two daughters, emigrated via Greenock aboard the Commerce of Greenock, Captain Covendale, bound for Quebec on 11 May 1821, was granted land in Lanark, Upper Canada, on 6 August 1821. [PAO] [TNA.CO42.189]

ANSTRUTHER, CHARLES, a skipper in Port Glasgow, testament, 1823, Comm. Glasgow, [NRS]

ARBUCKLE, SIMON, a merchant, was admitted as a burgess and guilds-brother of Glasgow on 3 April 1822. [GBR]

ARBUCKLE, ISABELLA, eldest daughter of S. Arbuckle a leather merchant in Glasgow, married James Scott the editor of the 'Montreal Herald' in Glasgow on 21 August 1828. [S.901.554]

ARMSTRONG, WILLIAM, son of William Armstrong a merchant in Glasgow, was admitted as a burgess of Glasgow on 24 August 1796, died in St Vincent on 22 September 1800. [GBR][GM.70.1214]

ARTHUR, JAMES, eldest son of Robert Arthur, a victualler in Glasgow, settled in North America by 1803. [NRS.CS17.1.22/78]

ARTHUR, JAMES, from Glasgow, died in St Mary's, Jamaica, on 6 March 1819. [S.3.122]

ARTHUR, THOMAS, from Glasgow, died in Lisbon, Portugal, in 1812. [EA5025] [SM.74.238]

AUCHINCLOSS, WILLIAM, a merchant of the firm Auchincloss and Robertson, merchants of 32 Glassford Street, Glasgow, was admitted as a burgess, and guilds-brother on 18 April 1815. [GBR]

AUCHENVOLE, ALEXANDER, in Kilsyth, dead by 1800, father of David Auchenvole, a merchant in New York. [NRS.S/H]

AULD, Reverend J. M., from Glasgow, died in Kingston, Jamaica, on 8 February 1851. [W.1202]

AYTON, JAMES, son of William Ayton, [1785-1845], and his wife Agnes Inglis, [1800-1878], settled in Oamaru, New Zealand. [Carnwath gravestone]

AYTON, WILLIAM, 1785-1845, husband of Agnes Inglis, 1800-1878, parents of James Ayton who settled in Oamaru, New Zealand. [Carnwath gravestone]

AITON, WILLIAM, a writer and messenger in Strathaven, versus Thomas Fleming, a labourer at Hoodstonesbridge, in 1790. [NRS.CS228.A6.5]

BABCOCK, B. F., from Glasgow, married Maria Augusta Bicknell, daughter of W. T. Bicknell, in Patterson, New Jersey, on 3 April 1844. [GEP.857]

BAIN, DUNCAN, of the Glasgow Canadian Emigration Society, with his wife and family, emigrated via Greenock aboard the George Canning, Captain Potter, bound for Quebec on 14 April 1821. [TNA.CO42.189]

BAIN, JOSEPH, of Morrisston, born 1761, died 28 April 1841, husband of Margaret Bell, born 1766, died 17 November 1806. [Ramshorn church crypt] of the Bridgeton Transatlantic Emigration Society, with his wife and family, emigrated via Greenock aboard the George Canning, Captain Potter, bound for Quebec on 14 April 1821. [TNA.CO42.189]

BAIN, ROBERT, a shipmaster in Port Glasgow, testament, 1798, Comm. Glasgow. [NRS]

BAIN, WALTER, of the Bridgeton Transatlantic Emigration Society, with his wife and family, emigrated via Greenock aboard the George Canning, Captain Potter, bound for Quebec on 14 April 1821. [TNA.CO42.189]

BAINIE, Mrs, of the Rutherglen Emigration Society, emigrated via Greenock aboard the Commerce of Greenock, Captain Covendale, bound for Quebec on 11 May 1821. [TNA.CO42.189]

BAIRD, ARCHIBALD, in Rutherglen, applied to settle in Canada on 3 March 1815. [NRS.RH9]

BAIRD, JOHN, master of the Three Sisters of Glasgow from Greenock to Boston, Massachusetts, in 1815. [NRS.E504.15.109]

BAIRD, JOHN, of the Glasgow Trongate Emigration Society, emigrated via Greenock aboard the David of London, master David Gemmil, bound for Quebec on 19 May 1821. [TNA.CO42.189]

BAIRD, ROBERT, of the Strathaven and Kilbride Emigration Society, with his wife and family, emigrated via Greenock aboard the George Canning, Captain Potter, bound for Quebec on 14 April 1821. [TNA.CO42.189]

BAIRD, ROBERT MACGREGOR, eldest son of Charles R. Baird in Glasgow, died near Golden City, British Columbia, in November 1884. [S.12971]

BAIRD, ROBERT, son of Robert Baird a lawyer in Glasgow, matriculated at Glasgow University in 1853, Judge of the District of Port Antonio in Jamaica, died in Kingston, Jamaica, on 11 October 1888. [MAGU]

BAIRD, WILLIAM, of the Strathaven and Kilbride Emigration Society, emigrated via Greenock aboard the George Canning, Captain Potter, bound for Quebec on 14 April 1821. [TNA.CO42.189]

BAIRD, WILLIAM, in Airdrie, father of Jessie Baird who married Jackson Miller in Singapore on 10 September 1884. [S.12846]

BALDERSTON, THOMAS, fourth son of David Balderston of HM Customs at Port Glasgow, died in Jamaica on 2 November 1821. [GkAd.27.6.1822]

BALFOUR, JOHN, a merchant in Glasgow, husband of Janet Corbett, late of Jamaica, was granted Kenmuir, 2 June 1813, and May 1814. [NRS.RGS.148.55; CS17.1.34/401]

BALLANTYNE, PATRICK, a merchant in Kingston, Jamaica, a witness in 1816; co-owner of the Mercury of Glasgow in 1795. [NRS.RD5.97.266; CE60.11.4/21]

BAN, JAMES, born 1812 in Glasgow, a planter in Charleston, South Carolina, was naturalised there on 3 February 1842. [NARA.M1183.1]

BANKHEAD, JAMES, of the Cathcart Emigration Society, emigrated via Greenock on board the Earl of Buckinghamshire, Captain Johnston, bound for Quebec on 29 April 1821, with his wife, four sons, was granted land in Lanark, Upper Canada, on 21 July 1821. [TNA.CO42.189] [PAO]

BANNATYNE, THOMAS, born 1773, a mariner from Glasgow, was naturalised in South Carolina on 6 September 1804. [NARA.M1173.1]

BANNATYNE, WILLIAM, from Lanark, a surgeon of the Royal Navy, testament, 1804, Comm. Lanark. [NRS]

BANNERMAN, Captain, master of the Favourite of Port Glasgow from the Clyde with passengers to Montreal and Quebec in 1840, 1841. [GA]

BARCLAY, ROBERT, of the Glasgow Trongate Emigration Society, with emigrated via Greenock aboard the David of London, master David Gemmil, bound for Quebec on 19 May 1821. [TNA.CO42.189]

BARCLAY, ROBERT, messenger at arms, Glasgow, 1849. [POD]

BARNS, WILLIAM, born 1845, son of Professor Islay Barns in Glasgow, died on 8 March 1870, buried in the British Cemetery, Funchal, Madeira. [ARM]

BARR, ALEXANDER, born in Glasgow, died in Georgia in 1801. [CMSA.11.12.1801]

BARR, ARCHIBALD, a farmer at Lynn of Cathcart, dead by 1812. [NRS.S/H]

BARR, DANIEL, born 1792, son of John Barr of Moat, [1757-1829], died in Jamaica in 1815. [Lesmahagow gravestone]

BARR, JAMES, a merchant in Port Glasgow, father of Robert Barr a merchant in Demerara in 1803. [NRS.S/H]

BARR, JAMES, of the Spring Bank Emigration Society, with his wife, son and daughter, emigrated via Greenock aboard the Commerce of Greenock, Captain Covendale, bound for Quebec on 11 May 1821, was granted land in Lanark, Upper Canada, on 8 August 1821. [TNA.CO42.189]

BARR, JOHN, of the Glasgow Loyal Agricultural Emigration Society, with his wife and family, emigrated via Greenock aboard the George Canning, Captain Potter, bound for Quebec on 14 April 1821. [TNA.CO42.189]

BARR, NEIL, of the Spring Bank Emigration Society, with his wife and two daughters, emigrated via Greenock aboard the Commerce of Greenock, Captain Covendale, bound for Quebec on 11 May 1821, was granted land in Lanark, Upper Canada, on 10 September 1821. [TNA.CO42.189] [PAO]

BARR, R., master of the Active of Glasgow bound from Greenock to Montreal, Quebec in 1816. [NRS.E504.15.111]

BARR, ROBERT, in Jamaica, son of Peter Barr in Hutchesontown, Glasgow, a letter, 1846. [GCA.GB23D1710]

BARR, WILLIAM, of the Hamilton Emigration Society, emigrated via Greenock on board the Commerce of Greenock, Captain Coverdale, bound for Quebec on 11 May 1821. [TNA.CO42.89]

BARR, Captain, master of the Brilliant of Glasgow from Glasgow to Quebec in 1844. [QM.20.6.1844], also in 1845. [QM.5.6.184]

BAXTER, PETER, of the North Albion Emigration Society, emigrated via Greenock on board the Commerce of Greenock, Captain Coverdale, bound for Quebec on 11 May 1821, was granted land in Lanark, Upper Canada, on 7 August 1821. [TNA.CO42.89] [PAO]

BEATTIE, WALTER, of the Abercrombie Emigration Society, with his wife and family, emigrated via Greenock aboard the David of London, master David Gemmil, bound for Quebec on 19 May 1821. [TNA.CO42.189]

BEGG, ARCHIBALD, born 1777, son of Hugh Begg, [who died in September 1786], and his wife Margaret Taylor, [died in May 1783], died in America in April 1816. [Lesmahagow gravestone]

BEGG, HUGH, born 1776, son of Hugh Begg, [who died in September 1786], and his wife Margaret Taylor, [died in May 1783], died in America in November 1806. [Lesmahagow gravestone]

BELL, ELIZABETH, from Glasgow, married John Campbell at Lanethall, Jamaica in 1790. [GM.60.1213]

BELL, GEORGE A., from New York, married Isabella Elizabeth Blakey, youngest daughter of Robert Blakey, Professor of Logic and Metaphysics at Queen's College, Belfast, in Symington, on 9 September 1850. [W.XL.1153]

BELL, JOHN, only son of James Bell in Jamaica, matriculated at Glasgow University in 1817. [MAGU]

BELL, JOHN, master of the Maid of the Mill of Port Glasgow from Port Glasgow to St John, New Brunswick, in 1818. [NRS.E504.28.101]

BELL, JOHN, in Lanark, father of James Bell who died in Ascuncion del Paraguay on 9 April 1870. [S.8347]

BELL, MATTHEW, a wright in Calton, testaments, 1795-1797, Comm. Glasgow. [NRS]

BELL, WILLIAM, a merchant in Port Glasgow, testaments, 1799, Comm. Glasgow. [NRS]

BELL, WILLIAM, son of William Bell a weaver in Anderston, was educated at Glasgow University from 1805, was ordained in Edinburgh on 4 March 1817, a minister in Perth, Canada. [MAGU] [AUPC]

BELL, WILLIAM, in Glasgow, applied to settle in Canada on 27 February 1815. [NRS.RH9]

BERRY, JAMES, a merchant in Jamaica, died in Glasgow, testament, 1817. [NRS.CC9.9.93]

BERRIE, ROBERT, a barrister at law from Glasgow, married Helen Eliza Butler, eldest daughter of Johnston Butler of Niagara, in Dundas, Gore, Upper Canada, on 11 March 1823. [SM.92.254]

BERTRAM, GEORGE, merchant in Biggar, testament, 22 March 1798, [NRS]

BERTRAM, JEAN, daughter of John Bertram, [1807-1878], and his wife Grace Muir, [1804-1855], wife of Charles Riddel, died in Canterbury, New Zealand, on 7 September 1865. [Biggar gravestone]

BERTRAM, JOHN, [1807-1878], and his wife Grace Muir, [1804-1855], parents of Jean who died in Canterbury, New Zealand, on 7 September 1865. [Biggar gravestone]

BERTRAM, ROBERT, in Dolphinbank, Dolphinton, was a victim of forgery and theft in 1850. [NRS.AD14.50.521]

BERTRAM, of Nisbet family, papers 1571 to 1890. [NRS.GD5]

BEVERIDGE, JAMES, of the Glasgow Wrights Emigration Society, with his wife and family, emigrated via Greenock aboard the George Canning, bound for Quebec on 14 April 1821. [TNA.CO42.189]

BIGGS, ADAM, late in Jamaica, died in Glasgow on 21 June 1798. [AJ.2633]

BIGGS, ARCHIBALD, from Lesmahagow, Lanarkshire, settled in Elizabeth, Essex County, New Jersey, probate 9 April 1816. [NJA.10961G]

BISSETT, ELISABETH, born 1801, relict of David Murdoch DD from Glasgow, died in Elmira, New York, on 29 August 1873. [GH.10521]

BISSLAND, JOHN, from Port Glasgow, died in Kingston, Jamaica, on 10 October 1817, he was a passenger on the Surprise of Glasgow which was wrecked on the coast of Mogadore. [S.1.49][GkAd.26.12.1817]

BIZZET, WILLIAM W., second son of Alexander Bizzet, a planter in Jamaica, matriculated at Glasgow University in 1847. [MAGU]

BLACK, GEORGE, son of John Black a merchant in Biggar, was apprenticed to George Goodlet, a saddler and beltmaker in Edinburgh, for six years, on 24 August 1797. [ERA]

BLACK, JAMES, in Parkhead, applied to settle in Canada on 4 March 1815. [NRS.RH9]

BLACK, JAMES, with five dependents, members of the Lesmahagow Emigration Society, were bound for Quebec in 1820. [TNA.CO384.10.1062]

BLACK, JAMES, of the Bridgeton Transatlantic Emigration Society, emigrated via Greenock aboard the George Canning, Captain Potter, bound for Quebec on 14 April 1821. [TNA.CO42.189]

BLACK, JAMES, a surgeon in Jamaica, later in Glasgow before 1835. [GA.0623.T.MJ.386.2]

BLACK, JOHN, born 1795 in Glasgow, died in Halifax, Nova Scotia, on 4 May 1820. [AR.6.5.1820]

BLACK, JOHN, born in Glasgow, of the firm of Watson, Black, and Company, died in Montreal, Quebec, on 10 August 1841. [AJ.4888]

BLACK, ROBERT, a surgeon in Jamaica, son of James Black a leather cutter and merchant in Glasgow, in 1799. [NRS.CS26.908.13]

BLACK, WALTER, President of the Glasgow Canadian Emigration Society, emigrated via Greenock aboard the George Canning, Captain Potter, bound for Quebec on 14 April 1821. [TNA.CO42.189]

BLACK, ..., from Glasgow aboard the Nancy bound for Jamaica, landed in Kingston in June 1793. [JRG.22.6.1793]

BLACKIE, WILLIAM, born 1792, a merchant from Glasgow who died in New York on 21 May 1823. [DPCA.1092][EEC.17474][SM.92.255]

BLACKWOOD, JOHN, son of John Blackwood of Ardsgreen, emigrated via Rothesay aboard the Fair Canadian bound for Quebec in June 1780. [NRS.NRAS.0067.1]

BLAIR, ANDREW, of the Glasgow Wrights Emigration Society, with his wife and family, emigrated via Greenock aboard the George Canning, Captain Potter, bound for Quebec on 14 April 1821. [TNA.CO42.189] 11

BLAIR, DAVID, born 1793, son of John Blair a calenderer in Glasgow, died in St Croix, Danish West Indies, on 3 February 1816. [Ramshorn gravestone, Glasgow]

BLAIR, ROBERT, fourth son of John Blair a merchant in Glasgow, died in Jamaica in 1817. [S.2.67]

BLAIR, THOMAS, sixth son of Thomas Blair a surgeon in Liberton, Lanarkshire, died in Jamaica on 10 October 1807. [SM.70.398]

BLAIR, WILLIAM, and his wife, of the Brownfield and Anderston Emigration Society, emigrated via Greenock on board the Earl of Buckinghamshire, Captain Johnston, bound for Quebec on 29 April 1821. [TNA.CO42.189]

BLYTH, HENRY, youngest son of John Blyth a planter in Jamaica, matriculated at Glasgow University in 1847. [MAGU]

BLYTH, JOHN, eldest son of John Blyth a merchant in Jamaica, matriculated at Glasgow University in 1830, graduated MD from Edinburgh University in 1839. [MAGU]

BOAG, ANDREW, in Bridgeton, Glasgow, applied to settle in Canada on 9 July 1819. [TNA.CO384.5.907]

BODIN, ALEXANDER, of the Rutherglen Emigration Society, and family emigrated via Greenock aboard the Commerce of Greenock, Captain Covendale, bound for Quebec on 11 May 1821. [TNA.CO42.189]

BOGLE, ANDREW, a merchant in Jamaica, co-owner of the Magnet of Glasgow in 1800; in Kingston, Jamaica in 1809; was granted land in Provan on 2 June 1817; a deed in 1820. [NRS.CE60.11.6/18; NRAS.0063; RGS.155.74; RD5.193.513]

BOGLE, PATRICK, of Hamilton Farm, Lanarkshire, and his son John Bogle, testaments, 1794-1795, Comm. Glasgow. [NRS]

BOGLE, ROBERT, jr., a merchant, was admitted as a burgess and guildsbrother of Glasgow on 6 November 1798, as eldest son of Archibald Bogle a merchant burgess and guilds-brother. [GBR]

BOGLE, ROBERT, born 1801, third son of Robert Bogle of Gilmorehill a merchant in Glasgow, died in Kingston, Jamaica, on 21 December 1819. [Kingston Cathedral gravestone, Jamaica] [S.4.161]

BOGLE, ROBERT, from Glasgow, a merchant in New Orleans, Louisiana, died in February 1826. [SM.97.640]

BOGLE, WILLIAM, of Gilmourhill, a merchant of 12 Queen Street, Glasgow, was admitted as a burgess and guilds-brother of Glasgow, on 8 January 1824, as eldest son of Robert Bogle a merchant, burgess and guilds-brother. [GBR]

BONE, ROBERT, son of John Bone a leadwasher at Leadhills, was apprenticed to Walter Russell, a merchant in Edinburgh, for five years on 10 May 1793. [ERA]

BOOTH, JAMES, of the Royal Navy, testament, 1817, Comm. Glasgow. [NRS]

BORDLAND, HUGH, a spirit dealer in Glasgow, testament, 1792, Comm. Glasgow. [NRS]

BORDLAND, JOHN, a farmer in Cowcaddens, testament, 1791, Comm. Glasgow. [NRS]

BORROWMAN, JAMES, President of the Barrowfield Road Emigration Society, with his wife and family, emigrated via Greenock aboard the

George Canning, Captain Potter, bound for Quebec on 14 April 1821. [TNA.CO42.189]

BORTHWICK, HECTOR GEORGE SINCLAIR, a merchant in Glasgow, died in Barcelona, Spain, testament, Glasgow, 1864. [NRS]

BOWES, ALEXANDER, of the Glasgow Trongate Emigration Society, emigrated via Greenock aboard the David of London, master David Gemmil, bound for Quebec on 19 May 1821. [TNA.CO42.189]

BOWES, JAMES, of the Glasgow Trongate Emigration Society, with his wife and family, emigrated via Greenock aboard the David of London, master David Gemmil, bound for Quebec on 19 May 1821. [TNA.CO42.189]

BOWES, JOHN, of the Glasgow Trongate Emigration Society, emigrated via Greenock aboard the David of London bound for Quebec on 19 May 1821.[TNA.CO42.189]

BOWES, THOMAS, of the Glasgow Trongate Emigration Society, emigrated via Greenock aboard the David of London, master David Gemmil, bound for Quebec on 19 May 1821. [TNA.CO42.189]

BOWIE, ALEXANDER, in Glasgow, a deed, 18 March 1841. [NRS.RD29.3.23]

BOWIE, HUGH, a mariner in Halifax, Nova Scotia, eldest son of William Bowie a weaver and former baillie of the Gorbals, later in Halifax, appointed James Richardson a merchant in Glasgow, and John Izat a maltman in the Gorbals, as his factors, on 12 May 1801. [NRS.RD3.289.569][NRS.S/H.1800]

BOWIE, WILLIAM, in Glasgow, testament, 1799, Comm. Glasgow. [NRS]

BOWMAN, ARCHIBALD, a merchant in New York who died in Glasgow in May 1790, testament, 3 November 1790, Comm. Glasgow. [NRS.CS17.1.23/84; CC9.7.74]

BOWMAN, JAMES, in Glasgow, son of George Melville a wright in Glasgow, testaments, 1793-1800, Comm. Glasgow. [NRS]

BOWMAN, JAMES, a hammerman, was admitted as a burgess and guilds-brother of Glasgow on 16 August 1820, as eldest son of Thomas Bowman a hammerman, burgess and guilds-brother. [GBR]

BOYD, ADAM, nephew of William Boyd in Townhead of Symington, settled in America by 1797. [NRS.CS16.1.16/132,177]

BOYD, JOHN, born in Glasgow, son of a minister, a merchant in Richmond, Virginia, in 1790. [DU.236/11.5.33]

BOYD, MARY, from Jamaica, married Robert Kalley, a merchant in Glasgow on 3 August 1795. [GM.65.702]

BOYD, THOMAS, a tailor, was admitted as a burgess and guilds-brother of Glasgow, on 13 June 1772, as husband of Elizabeth Wilson, daughter of John Wilson, a tailor burgess and guilds-brother; testament, 1797, Comm. Glasgow. [NRS][GBR]

BOYD, THOMAS, master of the Aurora of Glasgow from Greenock to Quebec and Montreal in 1803. [CM.12887]

BOYLE, WILLIAM, a meal dealer in Glasgow, testament, 1800, Comm. Glasgow. [NRS]

BRAID, HENRY, born 1745, a wright in Glasgow, died 9 May 1817. [Ramshorn gravestone]

BRAIDFUTE, JOHN, son of Reverend John Braidfute in Dunsyre, was apprenticed to John Bell, a bookseller in Edinburgh, for five years on 10 September 1793. [ERA]

BRAIDWOOD, ALEXANDER, son of William Braidwood a smith in Biggar, was apprenticed to William Braidwood, a merchant in Edinburgh, for five years, on 2 June 1796. [ERA]

BRAIDWOOD, JAMES, President of the Bridgeton Transatlantic Emigration Society, with his wife and family, emigrated via Greenock aboard the George Canning, Captain Potter, bound for Quebec on 14 April 1821. [TNA.CO42.189]

BRAND, WILLIAM, born 1761, a dyer in Glasgow, died 19 December 1814, husband of Janet McCubin, born 1763, died 22 November 1831. [Ramshorn gravestone]

BRASH, JOHN, a ploughman, with Catherine his wife and three children, in Port Dundas, bound for Canada in 1815. [TNA.CO385.2]

BRASH, Reverend JOHN, born 26 June 1824, son of Reverend William Brash, was educated at Glasgow University in 1844, settled in New York in 1854, died in South Amboy, New Jersey, on 21 March 1881. [ANY]

BRIGHT, JOHN, from Glasgow, died on passage to Port Natal, South Africa, in 1851. [W.1234]

BRODIE, JAMES, a saddletree maker and bailie of Glasgow, testament, 1792, Comm. Glasgow. [NRS]

BRODIE, JANET, born 1778, a spinner from Glasgow, with her son George Brodie, born 1804, emigrated via Oban aboard the Clarendon of Hull bound for Prince Edward Island in August 1808. [TNA.CO226.23]

BRODIE, WILLIAM, of Nervelston, testament, 1799, Comm. Glasgow. [NRS]

BROOKS, JAMES, of the Lesmahagow Emigration Society, with his wife, four sons, and two daughters, emigrated to Canada on the Earl of Buckinghamshire, Captain Johnston, on 29 April 1821, was granted land in Dalhousie, Upper Canada, on 20 July 1821. [TNA.CO42.189] [PAO]

BROOM, ALEXANDER, a builder in Glasgow, husband of Mary Rennie, born 1786, died 4 October 1827. [Ramshorn church crypt]

BROWN, AGNES, born 1801, daughter of Mackenzie Brown, [1769-1837], a farmer in Kirkhouse, and his wife Elizabeth Jamieson, [1780-1831], died in America on 19 October 1842. [Dolphinton gravestone]

BROWN, ALEXANDER, born 1829, a Presbyterian minister in Madeira, died there on 19 October 1857. [Lesmahagow gravestone] [ARM]

BROWN, ANDREW, of the Bridgeton Transatlantic Emigration Society, with his wife and family, emigrated via Greenock aboard the George Canning, Captain Potter, bound for Quebec on 14 April 1821. [TNA.CO42.189]

BROWN, BENJAMIN CORNWALL, born 9 November 1826 in Glasgow, son of James Brown, a dyer, and Catherine Moses his wife, was educated at the University of Glasgow, a minister of the West Chapel, from 1853 until his death on 1 October 1874. [F.3.221]

BROWN, DANIEL, from Port Glasgow, a shipmaster in Milford, Wales, in 1796. [NRS.S/H]

BROWN, DAVID, born 1795, son of Dr David Brown of St John, New Brunswick, died in Glasgow on 23 September 1810. [NBRG.4.2.1811]

BROWN, DAVID, from Glasgow, died in Jamaica in August 1822, inventory, 1835. [NRS.SC70.1.52]

BROWN, DAVID, born 1785, son of David Brown and his wife Helen Oswald, died in Jamaica on 2 January 1830. [Kingsbarns gravestone]

BROWN, DUNCAN, born 1752, an innkeeper in Halifax, Nova Scotia, died 1802, brother of David Brown in Glasgow, probate 10 August 1802, Halifax County, N.S.

BROWN, FRANCIS, born 1795 in Glasgow, son of James Brown, was educated at Glasgow University in 1807, a merchant in the West Indies, died in Jordanhill, Trinidad, on 15 November 1825. [MAGU]

BROWN, HUGH, from Hutchisontown, a divinity student in 1825, later emigrated to America. [AUPC]

BROWN, JAMES, a shipmaster in Port Glasgow, testament, 1792, Comm. Glasgow. [NRS]

BROWN, JAMES, President, of the Lesmahagow Emigration Society, with his wife and two sons, emigrated to Canada on the Earl of Buckinghamshire, Captain Johnston, on 29 April 1821, was granted land in Dalhousie, Upper Canada, on 3 September 1821. [TNA.CO42.189] [PAO]

BROWN, JAMES, in Dennistoun, a deed, 28 January 1841. [NRS.RD29.3.23]

BROWNE, JAMES, born 1785, died 9 February 1845, husband of Jane Smith, born 1793, died 2 April 1831, parents of James Browne, born 1814, died 21 May 1842. [Ramshorn church crypt]

BROWN, JOHN, clerk to Messrs Christie, Smith, and Company, merchants in Glasgow, testament, 1797, Comm. Glasgow. [NRS]

BROWN, JOHN, a merchant in Glasgow, testament, 1799, Comm. Glasgow. [NRS]

BROWN, JOHN, born 1776 in Dunsyre, son of William Brown [1750-1816] and his wife Margaret.....[1753-1823], died in Jamaica on 19 October 1804. [Dunsyre gravestone, Lanarkshire]

BROWN, JOHN, in Glasgow, applied to settle in Canada on 4 March 1815. [NRS.RH9]

BROWN, JOHN, from Glasgow, died in Halifax, Nova Scotia, on 12 September 1825. [AR.17.9.1825]

BROWN, MACKENZIE, a farmer in Kirkhouse, [1769-1837] and his wife Elizabeth Jamieson, [1780-1831], parents of Agnes Brown, born 1801, died in America on 19 October 1842. [Dolphinton gravestone]

BROWN, MARGARET, born 1810, wife of Robert Veitch, died in Adelaide, South Australia, on 27 September 1868. [Symington gravestone, Lanarkshire]

BROWN, MARY, daughter of William Brown a seedsman in Glasgow, and wife of Reverend Archibald MacLay, died in New York on 20 September 1848. [SG.1765]

BROWN, MATHEW, a shipmaster in Port Glasgow, testament, 1796, Comm. Glasgow. [NRS]

BROWN, RICHARD, master of the Mars of Port Glasgow from Tobermory, Mull, bound for Quebec and Pictou, Nova Scotia, in 1818. [NRS.E504.35.2]

BROWN, ROBERT, born 1763, a factor from Glasgow, was naturalised in South Carolina on 29 September 1812. [NARA.M1183.1]

BROWN, SAMUEL, born 1801, from Glasgow, died in Madeira on 30 November 1859. [Funchal gravestone][ARM]

BROWN, SIMON, a merchant was admitted as a burgess and guildsbrother of Glasgow on 21 October 1761, partner in the firm of Simon

Brown and Company, merchants in Glasgow, testaments, 1785-1787, Comm. Glasgow. [NRS][GBR]

BROWN, WILLIAM, fourth son of Laurence Brown in Edmonston, Lanarkshire, was educated at Glasgow University in 1774, died in Jamaica on 30 June 1811. [SM.73.798][MAGU][Car.4.5]

BROWNING, ARCHIBALD of the Camlachie Emigration Society, with his wife, two sons, and a daughter, emigrated via Greenock on board the Commerce of Greenock, Captain Coverdale, bound for Quebec on 11 May 1821, was granted land in Lanark, Upper Canada, on 1 August 1821. [TNA.CO42.89] [PAO]

BROWNING, MARY ANN, wife of James Jackson, late of Glasgow, died in Dumfries, Upper Canada, on 7 October 1838. [SG.721]

BROWNLIE, CATHARINE, in Hungryhill, testament, 1792, Comm. Glasgow. [NRS]

BROWNLIE, DAVID, of the Hamilton Emigration Society, emigrated via Greenock on board the Commerce of Greenock, Captain Coverdale, bound for Quebec on 11 May 1821, was granted land in Dalhousie, Upper Canada, on 15 July 1821. [TNA.CO42.89] [PAO]

BROWNLEE, JAMES, born 1801 near Glasgow, emigrated to America in 1827, settled in Mahony County, Ohio, a politician and abolitionist, died in Poland, Ohio, on 20 January 1879. [TSA]

BROWNLIE, JOHN, of the Hamilton Emigration Society, emigrated via Greenock on board the Commerce of Greenock, Captain Coverdale, bound for Quebec on 11 May 1821, was granted land in Dalhousie, Upper Canada, on 15 July 1821. [TNA.CO42.89] [PAO]

BROWNLIE, JOHN, born 1790 in Hamilton, died in Scarborough, Canada, on 6 July 1846. [W.VII.707]

BROWNLEE, MUNGO, a mason in Strathaven, Lanarkshire, in 1799. [NRS.CS228.B11.17]

BROWNLEE, WILLIAM CRAIG, born 1784 in Evandale, Lanarkshire, son of James Brownlee of Torfoot, a farmer, and his wife Margaret Craig, graduated from Glasgow University, MA in 1803, emigrated to America in 1808, DD in 1824, was naturalised in the Supreme Court of Pennsylvania on 20 April 1813, and in the Court of Common Pleas in Philadelphia on 23 May 1820, a pastor in Pennsylvania and in New Jersey, 1813-1817, Professor at Rutgers in 1825, a pastor in New York, died there on 10 February 1860, buried in the Second Street Cemetery, N.Y., husband of Maria MacDougall. [GG][ANY][MAGU][UPC]

BROWNLIE, WILLIAM, of the Hamilton Emigration Society, emigrated via Greenock on board the Commerce of Greenock, Captain Coverdale, bound for Quebec on 11 May 1821, was granted land in Dalhousie, Upper Canada, on 15 July 1821. [TNA.CO42.89] [PAO]

BRUCE, ALEXANDER, found guilty of stealing horses, was sentenced, in Glasgow, to transportation to the colonies for 14 years, on 25 April 1811. [AM.83.5.393]

BRUCE, JAMES, a shipmaster in Port Glasgow, testament, 1797, Comm. Edinburgh. [NRS]

BRUCE, JAMES, in Carstairs, discharged his executor Peter Bruce, a deed, a deed, 10 January 1841. [NRS.RD29.3.23]

BRUCE, JOHN, of the Bridgeton Canadian Emigration Society, with his wife and family, emigrated via Greenock aboard the George Canning, Captain Potter, bound for Quebec on 14 April 1821. [TNA.CO42.189]

BRYCE, AGNES, wife of Hugh Martin an engine-driver in Iowa, heir to her grand-mother Jean Grindlay, widow of John Finlay in Airdrie, Lanarkshire, who died on 26 October 1847. [NRS.S/H]

BRYCE, JOHN, son of Thomas Bryce, [1748-1837], and his wife Agnes Brown, [1763-1840], died in Toronto aged 89. [Symington gravestone]

BRYCE, WILLIAM, sr., President of the Camlachie Emigration Society, with his wife four son, and four daughters, emigrated via Greenock on board the Commerce of Greenock, Captain Coverdale, bound for Quebec on 11 May 1821, was granted land in Sherbrook, Upper Canada, on 1 August 1821. [TNA.CO42.89] [PAO]

BRYCE, WILLIAM, jr., of the Camlachie Emigration Society, emigrated via Greenock on board the Commerce of Greenock, Captain Coverdale, bound for Quebec on 11 May 1821, was granted land in Sherbrook, Upper Canada, on1 August 1821. [TNA.CO42.89] [PAO]

BRYDEN, JAMES, from Glasgow, a land surveyor in St Elizabeth's, Jamaica, in 1797. [NRS.NRAS.0623.TMJ.427, 26]

BRYDEN, JAMES, born 1811, son of David Bryden a millwright in Douglas, died in Trinidad on 21 December 1838. [SG.8.745]

BRYDEN, THOMAS, born 1805, son of Thomas Bryden and his wife Janet Valence, died in Spain in May 1837. [Biggar gravestone]

BRYDIE, WILLIAM NAPIER, in Richmond, Virginia, appointed Alexander Sharp in Glasgow as his attorney, on 27 June 1816. [NRS.RD5.123.124]

BUCHAN, ALEXANDER, born 1747 in Glasgow, son of .... Buchan and his wife Margaret Ramsay, died in Grenada on 5 May 1795. [Ramshorn gravestone, Glasgow]

BUCHAN, ROBERT, son of Robert Buchan in Chapel, Cambuslang, died in Tobago in 1817. [S.14.17]

BUCHAN, WALTER, from Glasgow, emigrated via Greenock aboard the Portaferry, bound for Quebec in May 1832. [QM.13.6.1832] [GWS]

BUCHANAN, ALEXANDER, a merchant tailor in Glasgow, testaments, 1792 - 1794, Comm. Glasgow. [NRS]

BUCHANAN, ANN, in Glasgow, daughter of Andrew Buchanan of Drumpelier, testament, 1796, Comm. Glasgow. [NRS]

BUCHANAN, ARCHIBALD, of the Rutherglen Emigration Society, with his wife, two sons, and two daughters, emigrated via Greenock aboard the Commerce of Greenock, Captain Covendale, bound for Quebec on 11 May 1821, was granted land in Lanark, Upper Canada, on 9 September 1821. [TNA.CO42.189] PAO]

BUCHANAN, DAVID CARRICK, of Mount Vernon and Drumpelier, a banker in Glasgow, was discharged as executor of Robert Pollock a merchant in Petersburg, Virginia, on 10 April 1823. [NRS.RD5.244.204]

BUCHANAN, GEORGE, son of Neil Buchanan, a merchant in London, testaments, 1790-1793, Comm. Glasgow. [NRS]

BUCHANAN, GEORGE, of Hillington, testament, 1797, Comm. Glasgow. [NRS]

BUCHANAN, GEORGE, a tanner from Glasgow, settled in Petersburg, Virginia, 1792, 1809. [NRS.CS17.1.12, 177; CS17.1.29/76]

BUCHANAN, JAMES, a servant and brewer to James McNair coalmaster at Greenfield, residing in High Carntyne, testament, 1799, Comm. Glasgow. [NRS]

BUCHANAN, JAMES, of the Rutherglen Emigration Society, emigrated via Greenock aboard the Commerce of Greenock, Captain Covendale, bound for Quebec on 11 May 1821, was granted land in Lanark, Upper Canada, on 9 September 1821. [TNA.CO42.189] [PAO]

BUCHANAN, JOHN, a chaise setter in Glasgow, testament, 1798, Comm. Glasgow. [NRS]

BUCHANAN, JOHN, born 1786 in Glasgow, a tallow chandler who emigrated via Greenock to America, was naturalised in New York on 4 March 1826. [NY Court of Common Pleas]

BUCHANAN, JOHN, a mason in Main Street, Gorbals, Glasgow, applied to settle in Canada on 10 March 1820. [NRS.CO384.6.103]

BUCHANAN, MARY, emigrated from Glasgow to New York by 1816. [NRS.CS17.1.35/196]

BUCHANAN, PETER, a vintner in Port Glasgow, testament, 1792, Comm. Glasgow. [NRS]

BUCHANAN, ROBERT, from Glasgow, settled in Maryland by 1790. [NRS.CS17.1.9/150]

BUCHANAN, THOMAS, born 24 December 1744 in Glasgow, son of George Buchanan, a maltman, and his wife Jean Lowden, was educated at Glasgow University, emigrated to New York in 1763, a merchant there, died on 10 September 1815. [ANY][NRS.RS54.PR36/308; CS17.1.23/124]

BUCHANAN, THOMAS, a farmer in Croftspar, Barony parish, later in Parkhead, testament, 1800, Comm. Glasgow. [NRS]

BUCHANAN, THOMAS, of the Lanarkshire Emigration Society, emigrated to Canada on the Earl of Buckinghamshire, Captain Johnston, on 29 April 1821, settled in Ramsay, Upper Canada, on 26 July 1821. [PAO][TNA.CO42.189]

BUCHANAN, THOMAS, a merchant of the firm Buchanan and Brothers in Candleriggs, was admitted as a burgess and guilds-brother of Glasgow on 2 September 1828, as younger son of James Buchanan of Dowanhill a burgess and guilds-brother. [GBR]

BUCHANAN, WALLIS, born 1827, second son of Robert Carrick Buchanan of Drumpellier, Lanarkshire, late of the 92nd Highlanders, died in Alexandria, Egypt, on 18 March 1855. [EEC.227719]

BUCHANAN, WILLIAM, a merchant from Glasgow, in Virginia by 1790. [NRS.CS17.1.9.115]

BUCHANAN, WILLIAM TRUEMAN, in New Zealand, grandson and heir of William Trueman, a ropemaker in Glasgow, and his wife Ann Morrison, 1840. [NRS.S/H]

BUNTEN, ROBERT, an iron merchant in Jamaica Street, Glasgow, was admitted as a burgess and guilds-brother of Glasgow, on 22 November 1824, as younger son of William Bunten an iron merchant, burgess and guilds-brother; father of Robert Bunten who settled in Australia before 1854. [NRS.S/H][GBR]

BURGESS, WILLIAM, born 1791, a labourer in Port Glasgow, emigrated via Port Glasgow aboard the Favourite of St John bound for St John, New Brunswick, on 22 October 1815. [PANB.ms.RS23E.9798]

BURGESS, ..., born 1794, a labourer in Port Glasgow, emigrated via Port Glasgow aboard the Favourite of St John bound for St John, New Brunswick, on 22 October 1815. [PANB.ms.RS23E.9798]

BURNET, JAMES, a hosier in Glasgow, testament, 1800, Comm. Glasgow. [NRS]

BURNETT, JAMES, a shoemaker, was admitted as a burgess and guilds-brother of Glasgow, on 9 August 1802. [GBR]

BURNETT, JOHN, master of the Penelope of Port Glasgow from Port Glasgow to Newfoundland in 1818. [NRS.E504.28.100]

BURNETT, JOHN, in Glasgow, a deed, 3 December 1841.
[NRS.RD29.3.23]

BURNS, ALAN, born 18 September 1781 in Glasgow, son of Reverend John Burns, a physician at the Russian Imperial Court, died on 24 June 1813. [F.3.394]

BURNS, ALEXANDER, a hammerman of Upper Buchanan Street, Glasgow, was admitted as a burgess and guilds-brother of Glasgow on 9 March 1826, as eldest son of Robert Burns, a hammerman, burgess and guilds-brother. [GBR]

BURNS, ANDREW, from Glasgow, a merchant in Melbourne, Australia, in 1853. [NRS.S/H]

BURNS, GEORGE, of Linnbank, born 1788 in Hamilton, died in Granville County, North Carolina, in 1843. [W.V.427][EEC.20982] [DGH.25.1.1844]

BURN, GEORGE, from St Kitts, third son of George Burn a coach proprietor in Glasgow, died in Greenock on 1 February 1849. [EEC.21769]

BURNS, JAMES, son of John Burns a tailor, in Hamilton, nephew of James Govan a wright in Jamaica, 1789. [NRS.S/H]

BURNS, JAMES, son of William Burns, an innkeeper in Hamilton, dead by 1808. [NRS.S/H]

BURNS, JAMES, born 1775 in Hamilton, died in Sterling, Cayuga County, New York, on 8 February 1845. [DGH.27.3.1845]

BURNS, JOHN, son of John Burns a tailor, in Hamilton, nephew of James Govan a wright in Jamaica, 1789. [NRS.S/H]

BURNS, JOHN, in Watson Mids, Cambusnethan, testament, 1800, Comm. Glasgow. [NRS]

BURNS, Dr ROBERT, born 9 November 1809 in Glasgow, was educated at Glasgow University, emigrated to Philadelphia, Pennsylvania, on 5 May 1828, graduated from the University of Pennsylvania on 5 April 1839, a physician who died in Frankford, Philadelphia on 12 March 1883. [AP]

BURNS, WILLIAM, in Bordenton, New Jersey, son of William Burns a vintner in Hamilton, subscribed to a deed in Bordenton, NJ, on 3 November 1806. [NRS.RD3.315.732]

BURNS, GAVIN, master of the Favourite of Port Glasgow from the River Clyde with passengers to Montreal and Quebec in 1833, 1834, 1835, 1836. [GA]; master of the Ann Rankin of Glasgow bound from Glasgow with passengers for Quebec in 1851. [SRA.T/CN.26.5]

BURNSIDE, JANET, widow of John Buchanan a weaver in Glasgow, testament, 1797, Comm. Glasgow. [NRS]

BURNSIDE, JOHN, born 1851, a merchant in Glasgow, died 13 October 1813, husband of Margaret Allan, born 1762, died 12 July 1808. [Ramshorn gravestone]

BURNSIDE, Captain, master of the Mars of Glasgow from Greenock to New Orleans, Louisiana, in 1821. [NRS.E504.15.138]

CAINIE, NEIL, born 1805, from Glasgow, died in Madeira on 8 November 1827. [ARM]

CAIRNS, ROBERT, a merchant, was admitted as a burgess and guilds-brother of Glasgow on 22 January 1826, having served an apprenticeship with David Balcanquel and Peter Henderson merchants, burgesses and guild-brothers. [GBR]

CALDER, JAMES, born 1790 in Glasgow, a cabinetmaker in Charleston, South Carolina, was naturalised on 1 September 1813. [NARA.M1183.1]

CALDER, JAMES, of the Bridgeton Canadian Emigration Society, with his wife and family, emigrated via Greenock aboard the George Canning, Captain Potter, bound for Quebec on 14 April 1821. [TNA.CO42.189]

CALDERHEAD, ALEXANDER, born 1750, son of John Calderhead in Carluke, educated at Glasgow University in 1777, minister at Horndean, Berwickshire, from 1787 to 1802, then in West Middleton, Pennsylvania, later in Ohio, from 1803 until his death on 31 January 1812. [MAGU][UPC]

CALDERHEAD, JOHN, a baker, was admitted as a burgess and guilds-brother of Glasgow on 17 April 1816, having served his apprenticeship with William Marshall a baker, burgess and guilds-brother. [GBR]

CALDERHEAD, WILLIAM, a wright and joiner in Glasgow, testament, 1797, Comm. Glasgow. [NRS]

CALDWALL, JOHN, of Auldyard, testament, 1799, Comm. Glasgow. [NRS]

CALDWELL, MARTIN, born 1797, from Glasgow, late of St Vincent, died in London, England, on 23 February 1838. [SG.750]

CAMERON, ARCHIBALD, a merchant was admitted as a burgess and guilds-brother of Glasgow on 15 April 1755, by right of his wife Mary Cameron daughter of John Cameron a merchant burgess and guilds-merchant. [GBR]; testament, 1793, Comm. Glasgow. [NRS]

CAMERON, HUGH, late of Glasgow, son of John Cameron of Carntyne, died in Jamaica in 1804. [AJ.2970]

CAMERON, JEMIMA FISHER, daughter of D.A. Cameron in Glasgow, married Humphrey Ewing Buchan, MD, from Toronto, Ontario, in New York on 2 August 1870. [S.8441]

CAMERON, JOHN, of Carntyne, was admitted as a merchant burgess and guilds-brother of Glasgow on 6 March 1766, testaments, 1790-1791, Comm. Glasgow. [NRS][GBR]

CAMERON, JOHN, second son of John Cameron of Carntyne, Barony, Glasgow, matriculated a Glasgow University in 1767, died in Jamaica in 1794. [MAGU]

CAMERON, JOHN, born 1815, a labourer in Abercromby Street, Calton, Glasgow, was accused of mobbing, rioting, theft, robbery and assault in 1850. [NRS.AD14.50.67]

CAMERON, PETER, from East Kilbride, emigrated via Greenock aboard the Portaferry, bound for Quebec in May 1832. [QM.13.6.1832] [GWS]

CAMERON, ROBERT, of the Glasgow Wrights Emigration Society, with his wife and family, emigrated via Greenock aboard the George Canning, Captain Potter, bound for Quebec on 14 April 1821. [TNA.CO42.189]

CAMPBELL, Major General ARCHIBALD, late Governor of Jamaica, was admitted as an honorary burgess and guilds-brother of Glasgow on 23 September 1784. [GBR]

CAMPBELL, ARCHIBALD, a merchant, late in Jamaica, died in Glasgow on 17 January 1820. [S.4.158]

CAMPBELL, ARCHIBALD, of the Rutherglen Emigration Society, emigrated via Greenock aboard the Commerce of Greenock, Captain Covendale, bound for Quebec on 11 May 1821. [TNA.CO42.189]

CAMPBELL, ARCHIBALD, from Glasgow, married Grace Victoria Gibson, youngest daughter of John Gibson, in New York on 15 November 1849. [SG.1879]

CAMPBELL, CHARLES, from Glasgow, a surgeon in the Service of the East India Company, died in Sumatra on 19 January 1808. [EEC.3.9.1808]

CAMPBELL, COLIN, the younger, formerly a merchant in Glasgow, later in Virginia in 1790. [NRS.CS17.1.9.60]

CAMPBELL, COLIN, a merchant formerly in Greenock, later, on Holland Estate, St Elizabeth's, Jamaica, a Process of Divorce versus Henrietta Campbell, daughter of Duncan Campbell, who were married in Glasgow in August 1776, in 1790. [NRS. Comm. Edinburgh]

CAMPBELL, COLIN, second son of Lauchlin Campbell an agent in Jamaica, matriculated at Glasgow University in 1846. [MAGU]

CAMPBELL, DANIEL, from Airdrie, was drowned in Lake Erie on 23 July 1850. [NRS.CC8.8.Inventory.1862]

CAMPBELL, DOUGALD, master of the Monarch of Glasgow from Greenock to New Orleans, Louisiana, in 1816. [NRS.E504.15.113]

CAMPBELL, DUNCAN, son of Dr Neil Campbell in Glasgow, a planter in Springfield Estate, Hanover, Jamaica, probate, 1803, London. [TNA.Pro.11.1388]

CAMPBELL, DUNCAN, the Collector of Excise in Glasgow, testaments, 1797-1799, Comm. Glasgow. [NRS]   26

CAMPBELL, DUNCAN, of the Rutherglen Emigration Society, with his wife, and two daughters, emigrated via Greenock aboard the Commerce of Greenock, Captain Covendale, bound for Quebec on 11 May 1821, was granted land in Sherbrook, Upper Canada, on 7 August 1821. [TNA.CO42.189] [PAO]

CAMPBELL, DUNCAN, eldest son of Reverend Alexander Campbell in St Andrew's, Jamaica, matriculated at Glasgow University in 1835. [MAGU]

CAMPBELL, GEORGE, a maltman in Glasgow, testament, 1790 Comm. Glasgow. [NRS]

CAMPBELL, HUGH, a hosier or tailor, was admitted as a burgess and guilds-brother of Glasgow on 19 February 1781, testament, 1799, Comm. Glasgow. [NRS][GBR]

CAMPBELL, HUGH, President of the Spring Bank Emigration Society, and family, emigrated via Greenock aboard the Commerce of Greenock, Captain Covendale, bound for Quebec on 11 May 1821, was granted land in Dalhousie, Upper Canada, on 3 September 1821. [TNA.CO42.189] [PAO]

CAMPBELL, ISOBEL, widow of Robert Dobson a teacher of mathematics in Glasgow, who had been admitted as a burgess and guilds-brother there on 22 May 1754, [GBR]; testament, 1792, Comm. Glasgow. [NRS]

CAMPBELL, JAMES, born 1776 in Glasgow, a cooper who died in Savanna, Georgia, on 13 June 1810. [Savanna Death Register]

CAMPBELL, JAMES, born on 6 August 1829 at Moor Park, Lanarkshire, son of James Murdoch Campbell and his wife Elizabeth Bogle, died at Mount Pleasant, St Vincent, on 14 May 1845. [Dean gravestone, Edinburgh]

CAMPBELL, JOHN, a merchant in Glasgow, testaments, 1800-1801, Comm. Glasgow. [NRS]

CAMPBELL, JOHN, of Campbell, Reeves, and Company in Glasgow, died in Trinidad on 24 August 1817. [S.I.42]

CAMPBELL, JOHN, of the Spring Bank Emigration Society, with his wife, four sons, and three daughters, emigrated via Greenock aboard the Commerce of Greenock, Captain Covendale, bound for Quebec on 11 May 1821, was granted land in Lanark, Upper Canada, on 6 September 1821. [TNA.CO42.189] [PAO]

CAMPBELL, JOHN, a merchant from Glasgow, settled in Montreal, Quebec, by 1823. [NRS.CS17.1.43/12]

CAMPBELL, JOHN, born 1792 in Glasgow, a merchant in Charleston, South Carolina, who was naturalised on 17 May 1825. [NARA.M1183.1]

CAMPBELL, JOHN, third son of Reverend John Campbell of Nicolson Secession Church in Lauriston, Glasgow, died in Kingston, Jamaica, in October 1837. [DPCA.1844]

CAMPBELL, JOHN, first son of Reverend Henry Campbell in Jamaica, matriculated at Glasgow University in 1850. [MAGU]

CAMPBELL, JOSEPH, of the Spring Bank Emigration Society, and his wife, emigrated via Greenock aboard the Commerce of Greenock, Captain Covendale, bound for Quebec on 11 May 1821, was granted land in Dalhousie, Upper Canada, on 8 August 1821. [TNA.CO42.189] [PAO]

CAMPBELL, JOSEPH, jr., from Glasgow, married Mary Abby Hague, only daughter of Reverend William Hague, DD, in Orange, New Jersey, on 2 July 1873. [EC.27695]

CAMPBELL, LAURENCE, from Glasgow, died in Charleston, South Carolina, in 1804. [AJ.2647]

CAMPBELL, MARGARET, relict of James Drew a maltman in Glasgow, testament, 1790, Comm. Glasgow. [NRS]

CAMPBELL, MARGARET HENRIETTA, wife of Samuel Magan a midshipman of the United States Navy, heir to Ralph Foster in Drummoyne, Lanarkshire, who died in February 1810. [NRS.S/H]

CAMPBELL, MARIA, relict of James Whyte in Glasgow, later in Jamaica, testament, 11 December 1804 Comm. Glasgow. [NRS]

CAMPBELL, PETER, born 1777 in Glasgow, a mariner who was naturalised in South Carolina on 16 June 1809. [NARA.M1183.1]

CAMPBELL, PETER, master of the Caledonia of Glasgow from Greenock to Newfoundland in 1815. [NRS.E504.15.107]

CAMPBELL, PETER MCGREGOR, a mariner in Broomielaw, testament, 1821, Comm. Glasgow. [NRS]

CAMPBELL, ROBERT, of the Spring Bank Emigration Society, with his wife, son, and three daughters, emigrated via Greenock aboard the

Commerce of Greenock, Captain Covendale, bound for Quebec on 11 May 1821, was granted land in Dalhousie, Upper Canada, on 3 September 1821. [TNA.CO42.189] [PAO]

CAMPBELL, THOMAS, a merchant in Grenada, appointed his brother, John Campbell sr., a merchant in Glasgow, as his factor and attorney, 23 March 1790. [NRS.RD2.257.479]

CAMPBELL, THOMAS, first son of John Campbell, formerly a merchant in Jamaica, matriculated at Glasgow University in 1845. [MAGU]

CAMPBELL, WILLIAM, youngest son of William Campbell of Queenshill, died in Philadelphia, Pennsylvania, on 22 June 1842. [EEC.20393]

CAMPBELL, Captain, master of the Three Bells of Glasgow from Glasgow with passengers bound for Quebec in 1853. [QM.6.9.1853]

CAMPSLIE, WILLIAM, in Blantyre, applied to settle in Canada on 28 February 1815. [NRS.RH9]

CANNON, THOMAS, and daughter, from Glasgow, emigrated via Greenock aboard the Portaferry, bound for Quebec in May 1832. [QM.13.6.1832] [GWS]

CARLIN, JOHN, born 26 May 1838 in Glasgow, educated in the Ratisbon Seminary, Germany, in 1852, ordained as a Roman Catholic priest, died in Scotland on 29 August 1870. [SIG.296]

CARMICHAEL, ARCHIBALD, born 1754 in Lanark, died in Stokes County, North Carolina, in 1828. [INC. 17075]

CARMICHAEL, JAMES, born 1775 in Glasgow, a merchant who was naturalised in South Carolina on 21 March 1803. [NARA.M1183.1]

CARNEGIE, JOHN, and family, from East Kilbride, emigrated via Greenock aboard the Portaferry, bound for Quebec in May 1832. [QM.13.6.1832] [GWS]

CARR, ANDREW, in Cowcaddens, Glasgow, a former sergeant of the Rifle Brigade, applied to settle in Canada on 10 September 1827. [TNA.CO384.5.785]

CARRICK, ROBERT, born 1802 in Glasgow, emigrated via Liverpool to America, was naturalised in New York on 9 May 1827. [NY Marine Court Records]

CARRICK, ROBERT, a cordiner, was admitted as a burgess and guildsbrother of Glasgow on 14 September 1824, as he had served an apprenticeship under James Notman a cordiner burgess and guildsbrother. [GBR]

CARRUTHERS, JAMES, in Lanark, a former soldier of the 21st Regiment of Foot, applied to settle in Canada on 16 April 1827. [TNA.CO384.5.775]

CARSE, JOHN, and family, from Glasgow, emigrated via Greenock aboard the Portaferry, bound for Quebec in May 1832. [QM.13.6.1832][GWS]

CARSEWELL, ROBERT, of the Cambuslang Emigration Society, emigrated via Greenock aboard the George Canning, Captain Potter, bound for Quebec on 14 April 1821. [TNA.CO42.189]

CASSELS, JOHN, [1817-1887], and his wife Agnes Cadzow, [1819-1887], parents of David Cassels who died in New Zealand in 1883. [Lanark gravestone]

CAVAN, ROBERT, in Glasgow, a deed, 19 October 1841. [NRS.RD29.3.23]

CHALMERS, ALEXANDER WHITE, in Lesmahagow, only child of David Chalmers in Richmond, Virginia, testament, 1820. [NRS.CC14.5.19.20/277]

CHALMERS, Mrs JOHN, a widow from Broomfield, Glasgow, died in Philadelphia, Pennsylvania, on 13 August 1819. [EA.5833]

CHALMERS, ROBERT, President of the Hamilton Emigration Society, with his wife, two sons, and four daughters, emigrated via Greenock on board the Commerce of Greenock, Captain Coverdale, bound for Quebec on 11 May 1821, was granted land in Dalhousie, Upper Canada, on 15 July 1821. [TNA.CO42.89] [PAO]

CHALMERS, THOMAS, born 1839, son of James Chalmers and his wife Christina Martin, died in Melbourne, Australia, on 25 January 1858. [Lanark gravestone]

CHAPMAN, Dr NATHANIEL, of Philadelphia, Pennsylvania, was admitted as a burgess and guilds-brother of Ayr on 4 October 1802. [ABR]

CHAPMAN, SAMUEL, born 1779, son of James Chapman, born 1733, died 1798, a farmer in Ponfeigh, Carmichael, and his wife Jane ....., born 1740-1814, died in Charleston, South Carolina, on 8 September 1806. [Carmichael gravestone]

CHARLES, MATTHEW, in Hitchenbrook, Montreal, Quebec, married Hannah McKeich, younger daughter of Peter McKeich in Port Glasgow on 21 July 1831. [AJ.4366],

CHARTERS, GEORGE, of the Glasgow Wrights Emigration Society, with his wife and family, emigrated via Greenock aboard the George Canning, Captain Potter, bound for Quebec on 14 April 1821. [TNA.CO42.189]

CHARTERS, Captain, master of the Thetis of Glasgow from Greenock to Halifax, Nova Scotia, and Miramachi, New Brunswick, in 1820. [NRS.E504.15.127]

CHESTNUT, JANET, daughter of Robert Chestnut in Hamilton, Lanarkshire, married Daniel Johnston, a merchant in Wakefield, Carleton County, New Brunswick, on 14 July 1832, in St John, N.B. [NBC.14.7.1832]

CHISHOLM, DANIEL, a carver, gilder, and wright, was admitted as a burgess and guilds-brother of Glasgow on 1 March 1811, having served his apprenticeship under James Bannerman a wright, burgess and guilds-brother. [GBR]

CHRISTAL, JOHN, a sailor in Glasgow, in 1790. [NRS.S/H]

CHRISTIE, JOHN, from Glasgow, late at Brigus, Conception Bay, Newfoundland, administration, 1817. [RGNA.23.9.1817]

CHRISTIE, JOHN, MD, from Glasgow, died in Havanna, Cuba, on 15 June 1818. [AJ.3683]

CHRISTISON, JAMES, messenger at arms, Glasgow, 1849. [POD]

CHRYSTAL, ROBERT, born 1815, youngest son of William Chrystal in Glasgow, matriculated at Glasgow University in 1829, later a merchant in Jamaica. [MAGU]

CHRYSTAL, WILLIAM, born 1801 in Stirling, son of William Chrystal the Rector of Glasgow Grammar School, and his wife Jean McEwan, was educated at Glasgow University in 1814, died in Missouri in 1858. [MAGU][Glasgow Cathedral plaque]

CLAFFORD, Mr, from Glasgow aboard the Betsy and Brothers bound for Jamaica, landed in Kingston in May 1793. [JRG.25.5.1794]

CLARK, AGNES, born 1834, eldest daughter of Robert Clark, a builder in Glasgow, died at Montego Bay, Jamaica, on 27 October 1857. [Montego Bay gravestone]

CLARK, ISABELLA, relict of Charles McAlpine a painter in Glasgow, , testament, 1798, Comm. Glasgow. [NRS]

CLARK, JANET, relict of Peter Robertson a shoemaker in Glasgow who was admitted as a burgess and guilds-brother there on 7 September 1786, [GBR], testament, 1793, Comm. Glasgow. [NRS]

CLARK, JEMIMA, born 1799, wife of Robert Craig, died in Papanui, Auckland, New Zealand, on 6 June 1884. [Biggar gravestone]

CLARK, THOMAS, of 16 Nicolson Street, Launceston, Secretary of the Emigration Society of Glasgow, applied to settle in Canada on 10 October 1827. [TNA.CO384.5.793]

CLARK, WILLIAM, a mariner in Glasgow, testament, 1798, Comm. Glasgow. [NRS]

CLERK, WILLIAM, born in Jamaica, only son of William Clark formerly a vicar, matriculated at Glasgow University in 1811. [MAGU]

CLELAND, JAMES, in Glasgow, was admitted as a burgess and guilds-brother of Ayr on 27 January 1812. [ABR]

CLELLAND, JAMES, LLD, born 1770, died 14 October 1840, father of Henry Wilson Clelland, MD, born 1816, died 30 October 1844. [Ramshorn church crypt]

CLELAND, JOHN, born 1807 in Glasgow, an agriculturalist who settled in the Swan River colony, Western Australia, on 3 August 1830. [BPP.3.440/454]

CLIENCOFF, JOHN, a weaver in Glasgow, son of Jacob Cliencoff, a sugar baker in Glasgow, and his wife Mary Lawson, was admitted as a burgess and guilds-brother of Ayr on 24 April 1822, by right of his mother Mary Lawson, daughter of Hugh Lawson, a cooper burgess and guilds-brother of Ayr. [ABR]

CLIMIE, ANDREW, of the Govan Emigration Society, with his wife, five sons, and two daughters, emigrated via Greenock on board the Commerce of Greenock, Captain Coverdale, bound for Quebec on 11 May 1821, was granted land in Dalhousie, Upper Canada, on 1 August 1821. [TNA.CO42.89] [PAO]

CLOSS, JOHN, of the Brownfield and Anderston Emigration Society, emigrated via Greenock on board the Earl of Buckinghamshire, Captain Johnston, bound for Quebec on 29 April 1821, with his son and daughter, was granted land in Lanark, Upper Canada, on 21 July 1821. [TNA.CO42.189] [PAO]

CLOW, JAMES, of Duchally, Professor of Philosophy at Glasgow University, testament, 1799, Comm. Glasgow. [NRS]

CLUGSTON, AGNES, widow of Alexander Hewhand a merchant in Glasgow, who was admitted as a burgess and guilds-brother of Glasgow on 4 October 1763, [GBR]; testament, 1791, Comm. Glasgow. [NRS]

COATS, GEORGE, formerly in St John's, New Brunswick [?], later in Glasgow by 1823. [NRS.CS17.1.42/15]

COBB, JOHN, of the St John's Parish Emigration Society, with his wife, two sons and two daughters, emigrated via Greenock aboard the Commerce of Greenock, Captain Covendale, bound for Quebec on 11 May 1821, was granted land in Ramsay, Upper Canada, on 10 September 1821. [TNA.CO42.189] [PAO]

COCHRANE, JAMES, a smith in Rutherglen, testament, 1791, Comm. Glasgow. [NRS]

COCHRANE, JAMES, of the Rutherglen Emigration Society, with his wife, three sons and three daughters, emigrated via Greenock aboard the Commerce of Greenock, Captain Covendale, bound for Quebec on 11 May 1821, was granted land in Lanark, Upper Canada, on 10 September 1821. [TNA.CO42.189] [PAO]

COCHRANE, JOHN, a merchant in Glasgow, testament, 1794, Comm. Glasgow. [NRS]

COCHRANE, J., in Rutherglen, applied to emigrate to Canada on 3 March 1815. [NRS.RH9]

COCHRANE, WILLIAM, secretary to the Earl of Eglinton, at Coilsfield, testament, 1799, Comm. Glasgow. [NRS]

COCK, DANIEL, born 1718 in Roberton, Clydesdale, educated at Glasgow University in 1744, minister of Cartsdyke in 1752, emigrated in 1771, minister in Truro, Nova Scotia, from 1772 until 1798, died 17 March 1805. [NSRG.28.3.1805][MAGU.31][HPC]

COLLINGWOOD, JOHN, born 1810 in Glasgow, a grocer who was naturalised in South Carolina on 19 July 1839. [NARA.M1183.1]

COLLINS, EDWARD, born 1795, died 5 July 1864, husband of Susanna Heywood, born 1795, died 9 September 1882, parents of Juliet, born 1834, died in January 1839. [Ramshorn church crypt]

COLLINS, Captain, of the Rebecca of Glasgow, from the River Clyde to Pictou, Nova Scotia, in 1856. [GA]

COLQUHOUN, ANGUS, of the Bridgeton Transatlantic Emigration Society, with his wife and family, emigrated via Greenock aboard the George Canning, to Quebec on 14 April 1821. [TNA.CO42.189]

COLQUHOUN, CECILIA, wife of James Kirkwood a grocer from Glasgow, later in America in 1806. [NRS.CS17.1.25/475]

COLQUHOUN, DUNCAN, born 1837 in Glasgow, emigrated to America in 1856, declared his intention to naturalise on 21 November 1860. [Norfolk County Circuit Court Records, Virginia]

COLQUHOUN, HUGH, a mason in Rutherglen, when legally married to Isobel Kennedy at Broomielaw Quay, Anderson, bigamously married Jean Todd a widow in Mill Wynd, Rutherglen, in 1837.
[NRS.AD14.37.321]

COLQUHOUN, JAMES, of the Bridgeton Transatlantic Emigration Society, with his wife and family, emigrated via Greenock aboard the George 34 Canning, Captain Potter, bound for Quebec on 14 April 1821.
[TNA.CO42.189]

COLQUHOUN, MARGARET, widow of Robert Barbour a merchant in Glasgow, who was admitted as a burgess and guilds-brother of Glasgow on 5 July 1779, as younger son of Robert Barbour a weaver, burgess and guilds-brother, [GBR]; testament, 1795, Comm. Glasgow. [NRS]

COLQUHOUN, MARGARET, widow of David Dalziell a merchant in Glasgow, testament, 1799, Comm. Glasgow. [NRS]

COLVILLE, GEORGE, second son of George Colville a bookbinder in Glasgow, died on Nevis on 30 December 1838. [SG.70623.TMJ.427, 261]

CONNAGHAN, JOSEPH, born 5 May 1835 in Glasgow, educated in the Ratisbon Seminary, Germany, in 1852, ordained as a Roman Catholic priest, died in Glasgow on 18 January 1877. [SIG.296]

CONNAL, ALEXANDER, from Glasgow, emigrated via Greenock aboard the Portaferry, bound for Quebec in May 1832. [QM.13.6.1832] [GWS]

CONNELL, DAVID, a planter in Westmoreland, Jamaica, son of Provost Arthur Connell of Glasgow, in Glasgow in 1797.
[NRS.NRAS.0623.tmj.427/261]

CONNELL, JAMES, sr., a merchant in Glasgow, testament, 1792, Comm. Glasgow. [NRS]

CONNEL, WILLIAM, born 1780, a labourer in Port Glasgow, emigrated via Port Glasgow aboard the Favourite of St John bound for New Brunswick on 22 October 1815. [PANB.ms.RS23E.19798]

CONROY, EDWARD, with family of six members of the Lesmahagow Emigration Society in Lanark, bound for Quebec in 1820.
[TNA.CO384.6.101062]

COOK, ROBERT, tenant in Gilbertsfield, Cambuslang, testaments, 1793-1795, Comm. Glasgow. [NRS]

COOKE, WILLIAM, born 1794, eldest son of William Cooke the Rector of Hamilton Grammar School, died in Augustura on the River Orinocco, Venezuela, in 1820. [GkAd.2379]

COOPER, JAMES, a mariner and gabartman in Port Glasgow, testament, 1820, Comm. Glasgow. [NRS]

CORBETT, JANET, relict of John Balfour a merchant in Glasgow, later in Jamaica, was granted the lands of Kenmuir on 2 June 1813. [NRS.RGS.148/55]

COUPAR, ALEXANDER, a merchant in Glasgow, testament, 1796, Comm. Glasgow. [NRS]

COUPAR, WILLIAM, a merchant in Glasgow, testament, 1793, Comm. Glasgow. [NRS]

COUSIN, JANET, spouse of William Lisle a carter in Shettleston, testament, 1799, Comm. Glasgow. [NRS]

CRAIG, ANDREW, an ironmonger in Glasgow, testament, 1796, Comm. Glasgow. [NRS]

CRAIG, ANDREW, partner in the firm Andrew Craig and Company merchants in Millar Street, Glasgow, was admitted as burgess and guilds-brother of Glasgow on 12 July 1817, as eldest son of James Craig a weaver and manufacturer, burgess and guilds-brother. [GBR]

CRAIG, DAVID MATHIE, an apprentice writer in Glasgow, prepared a disposition for James McGill, and James Dunlop, merchants in Montreal, Quebec, in 1809. [NRS.RD5.221.255]

CRAIG, JAMES, a skipper in Port Glasgow, testament, 1807, Comm. Glasgow. [NRS]

CRAIG, JAMES, of the Brownfield and Anderston Emigration Society, emigrated via Greenock on board the Earl of Buckinghamshire, Captain Johnston, bound for Quebec on 29 April 1821. [TNA.CO42.189]

CRAIG, ROBERT, a shopkeeper in Glasgow, testament, 1798, Comm. Glasgow. [NRS]

CRAIG, ROBERT, of the Camlachie Emigration Society, with his wife, three sons, and a daughter, emigrated via Greenock on board the Commerce of Greenock, Captain Coverdale, bound for Quebec on 11 May 1821, was granted land in Lanark, Upper Canada, on 1 August 1821. [TNA.CO42.89] [PAO]

CRAIG, ROBERT, master of the New York of Glasgow from Glasgow with passengers to New York in 1858. [NARA.N237.181]

CRAIG, THOMAS, President of the Brownfield and Anderston Emigration Society, emigrated via Greenock on board the Earl of Buckinghamshire, Captain Johnston, bound for Quebec on 29 April 1821, with his son and daughter, was granted land in Ramsay, Upper Canada, on 26 July 1821. [TNA.CO42.189] [PAO]

CRAIGIE, LAURENCE, eldest son of Laurence Craigie a merchant in Jamaica, matriculated at Glasgow University in 1826. [MAGU]

CRAWFORD, ADAM, born 1784, a pocket book manufacturer in Glasgow, died 15 June 1843. [Ramshorn gravestone]

CRAWFORD, ANDREW, son of John Crawford a merchant in Port Glasgow, a merchant in St John, Newfoundland, in 1816. [NRS.SC53.56.1/82]

CRAWFORD, ANDREW, MD, from Port Glasgow, was drowned in the River St Lawrence, near Montreal, Quebec, on 15 August 1846. [W.VII.717]

CRAWFORD, GEORGE, a merchant was admitted as a burgess and guilds-brother of Glasgow on 18 September 1777 as eldest son of George Crawford a weaver burgess and guilds-brother, testament, 1799, Comm. Glasgow. [NRS][GBR]

CRAWFORD, GEORGE, from Glasgow, a merchant in Jamaica, testament, 4 January 1802. [NRS]

CRAWFORD, GEORGE, a writer in Glasgow, versus Robert Kerr a wright in Rutherglen, in 1804. [NRS.CS228.Misc.1/19]

CRAWFORD, JOHN, and Company, merchants in Port Glasgow and in Newfoundland, sederunt books, 1816-1826. [NRS.CS96.335.-340]

CRAWFORD, JOHN, of the Hamilton Emigration Society, with his wife, two sons, and two daughters, emigrated via Greenock on board the Commerce of Greenock, Captain Coverdale, bound for Quebec on 11 May 1821, was granted land in Dalhousie, Upper Canada, on 4 August 1821. [TNA.CO42.89] [PAO]

CRAWFORD, MATTHEW, a merchant from Paisley, was admitted as a burgess and guilds-brother of Glasgow on 3 February 1790, testament, 1794, Comm. Glasgow. [NRS][GBR]

CRAWFORD, MATTHEW, eldest son of John Crawford a surgeon in Glasgow, of Gifford Hall, St Elizabeth's, Jamaica, matriculated at Glasgow University in 1762, died in Teviot Row, Edinburgh, on 25 April 1815. [MAGU]

CRAWFORD, RALPH, born 1754, a merchant in Glasgow, died 14 July 1828, husband of Isabella Paterson, born 1770, died 14 October 1828. [Ramshorn gravestone]

CRAWFORD, RICHARD, in Jamaica, appointed his brother George Crawford, a writer in Glasgow, as his factor, on 13 June 1787. [NRS.RD2.243.329]

CRAWFORD, ROBERT, a yarn merchant in Rutherglen, testament, 1792, Comm. Glasgow. [NRS]

CRAWFORD, RONALD, of Friskyhall, a merchant was admitted as a burgess and guilds-brother of Glasgow on 7 May 1776, testament, 1793, Comm. Glasgow. [NRS][GBR]

CRAWFORD, STEPHEN R., born 22 January 1798, a merchant in Calcutta, India, who married Jane Wilson in Scotland in 1838, emigrated to Philadelphia, Pennsylvania, in 1840, died in Fox Chase, Philadelphia, on 28 April 1864. [AP]

CRAWFORD, THOMAS, son of Thomas Crawford a plasterer in Glasgow, was apprenticed to Andrew Irvine, a mason in Edinburgh, for six years, on 26 July 1798. [ERA]

CRAWFORD, WILLIAM, a skipper in Port Glasgow, testament, 1812, Comm. Glasgow. [NRS]

CRAWFORD, Captain, master of the Favourite of Port Glasgow from the River Clyde with passengers to Montreal and Quebec in 1847. [GA]

CREE, CLELAND, son of John Cree a nurseryman in Lanark, died at Montego Bay, Jamaica, on 10 October 1838. [Lanark gravestone]

CREE, WILLIAM, son of John Cree and his wife Mary Aitken in Lanark, died in Potose, Jamaica, on 6 August 1833. [Lanark gravestone]

CREIGHTON, WILLIAM, of the Barrowfield Road Emigration Society, with his wife and family, emigrated via Greenock aboard the George Canning, Captain Potter, bound for Quebec on 14 April 1821. [TNA.CO42.189]

CROMBIE, HUGH, of Humphrey Crombie and Company, merchants in Glasgow, a merchant and clerk in New York in 1807. [NRS.CS235.seqn.C2/2]

CROMBIE, JAMES, a weaver, was admitted as a burgess and guilds-brother of Glasgow on 16 February 1797. [GBR]

CROOM, WILLIAM, of the Barrowfield Road Emigration Society, with his wife and family, emigrated via Greenock aboard the George Canning, Captain Potter, bound for Quebec on 14 April 1821. [TNA.CO42.189]

CROSS, ELIZABETH, wife of John Muir a shoemaker in Cambuslang, in 1788, brother of James Cross in Virginia. [NRS.S/H]

CROSS, JANET, wife of William Shiels a farmer in Shiels, in 1788, brother of James Cross in Virginia. [NRS.S/H]

CROSS, ROBERT, of Barrachnie, residing in Glasgow, testament, 1795, Comm. Glasgow. [NRS]

CRUICKSHANK, JAMES, from Glasgow, married Martha Dyer, in Loda, New Jersey, on 27 May 1860. [S.1557]

CUMIN, PATRICK, born 1781, eldest son of Professor Cumin of Glasgow University, died in Egypt in 1802. [AJ.2829]

CUMMINGS, ARCHIBALD, of the Bridgeton Canadian Emigration Society, emigrated via Greenock aboard the George Canning, Captain Potter, bound for Quebec on 14 April 1821. [TNA.CO42.189]

CUMMING, ELIZABETH, widow of Dugald McFarlane a boatman in Glasgow, testament, 1793, Comm. Glasgow. [NRS]

CUMMINGS, GEORGE, of the Bridgeton Canadian Emigration Society, with his wife, emigrated via Greenock aboard the George Canning, Captain Potter, bound for Quebec on 14 April 1821. [TNA.CO42.189]

CUNNINGHAM, ALEXANDER, of the Lesmahagow Emigration Society, emigrated to Canada on the Earl of Buckinghamshire, Captain Johnston, on 29 April 1821. [TNA.CO42.189]

CUNNINGHAM, ANDREW, born 1828, son of William Cunningham, [1794-1864], and his wife Margaret Anderson, died in New York on 4 September 1862. [Govan gravestone]

CUNNINGHAM, ARCHIBALD, from Glasgow, died in New York on 13 September 1799. [AJ.2704]

CUNNINGHAM, ELIZABETH, daughter of James Cunningham of Jocley's Barn, Jamaica, married Reverend John Thomson, in Hamilton on 18 September 1845. [W.609]

CUNNINGHAM, JAMES, born 1801 in Govan, emigrated to USA in 1823, settled in New York, Boston, and San Francisco, a mechanical engineer and ship-owner, died in Irvington-on-Hudson, New York, on 28 April 1870. [ANY]

CUNNINGHAM, PETER, from Springfield, Glasgow, a stonecutter, a volunteer for Garibaldi in Italy in 1860. [SHR.57.169]

CUNNINGHAM, ROBERT, third son of Reverend Richard Cunningham in Symington, settled in Blandford, Virginia, died in 1796. [HCA]

CUNNINGHAM, WILLIAM, a spirit dealer and brush maker in Glasgow, testaments, 1794-1795, Comm. Glasgow. [NRS]

CUNNINGHAM, WILLIAM, a gabartman in Port Glasgow, testament, 1795, Comm. Glasgow. [NRS]

CUNNINGHAM, WILLIAM, from Glasgow, died in Trinidad on 3 October 1819. [EEC.16971]

CURRIE, GILBERT E., born 31 December 1818 in Glasgow, emigrated to USA in 1853, a publisher in New York from 1854 to 1859, died on 22 November 1882. [ANY]

CURRIE, JOHN, messenger at arms, Lanark, 1849. [POD]

CURTIS, RICHARD, jr., merchant of Curtis and Malcolm auctioneers in London Street, Glasgow, was admitted as a burgess and guilds-brother of Glasgow on 1 September 1828, as eldest son of Richard Curtis, a hammerman, burgess and guilds-brother. [GBR]

CUTHBERTSON, ALEXANDER, from Glasgow, emigrated via Greenock aboard the Portaferry, bound for Quebec in May 1832. [QM.13.6.1832] [GWS]

CUTHBERTSON, Reverend JOHN, born 1720 in Carnwath, ordained at Braehead in 1747, emigrated to America in 1752, died on 10 March 1791. [RPC.79]

CUTHBERTSON, WILLIAM, died 1814, husband of Janet MacDonald died 1867, parents of Donald died 1864, Janet died 1867, Agnes died 1874, and Allan died 1864. [Ramshorn church]

DALGLEISH, ROBERT, born 1770, died in 1844, husband of Jane Clyde, born 1770, died 1834. [Ramshorn church crypt]

DALGLEISH, SIMON, born 1790 probably in Glasgow, emigrated to USA in 1817, a commission agent in New York, died on 21 January 1819. [ANY]

DALRYMPLE, WILLIAM, died in Iter Boreale, St George's, Jamaica, on 25 December 1793. [Kirkintilloch gravestone]

DAVIE, ARCHIBALD, and Margaret Smith, both from Dalziel, were married in New York on 19 May 1798, he was a merchant there by 1803. [ANY] [NRS.CS17.1.22/488]

DAVIE, JEAN, found guilty of theft and sentenced in Glasgow to seven years transportation to the colonies in 1815. [NRS.GD1.959]

DAVIE, ROBERT, a gabartman in Newark, testament, 1817, Comm. Glasgow. [NRS]

DAVIS, ISAAC, master of the Isabella of Port Glasgow from Port Glasgow to St John, New Brunswick, in 1820. [NRS.E504.28.108]

DAW, WILLIAM, master of the Caledonia of Glasgow from Greenock to Newfoundland in 1815. [NRS.E504.15.109]

DEACHMAN, THOMAS, of the Glasgow Trongate Emigration Society, with his wife and family, emigrated via Greenock aboard the David of London, master David Gemmil, bound for Quebec on 19 May 1821. [TNA.CO42.189]

DEANE, MARIA, eldest daughter of Robert Deane a wine merchant in Glasgow, married Henry Heaton Bury from New York, in Glasgow in 1856. [CM.20734]

DEANS, JOHN, born 1823, formerly a gardener in Kinmount, died in Astoria, Long Island, New York, in 1869. [AO]

DENHOLM, JOHN, late in Quebec, died in Blythswood on 2 January 1831. [AJ.43341]

DENNISTON, JAMES, a banker in Glasgow, an attorney of William Wilson, a merchant in New York, 1816. [NRS.RD5.85.713]

DENNISTOUN, JAMES, born 1758, died 1836, husband of Maria Anna Bennett, born 1783, died 1836, parents of Anna, born 1816, died 1840. [Ramshorn church crypt]

DEWAR, JOHN, a merchant or grocer at 379 Gallowgate, Glasgow, was admitted as a burgess and guilds-brother of Glasgow on 3 December 1823, emigrated to America around 1827. [NRS.CS44.1827][GBR]

DEWAR, PLUMMER, born 1814, second son of Robert Dewar a merchant in Jamaica, matriculated at Glasgow University in 1830, died in Hamilton, Ontario, on 4 November 1878. [MAGU]

DEWAR, ROBERT, first son of Robert Dewar a merchant in Jamaica, matriculated at Glasgow University in 1827. [MAGU]

DICK, DAVID, a merchant in Jamaica, co-owner of the Mercury of Glasgow in 1795. [NRS.CE60.11.4/21]

DICK, JAMES BROWNLEE, born 23 March 1816 in Carluke, son of James Dick and Margaret Brownlee, married Margaret Dewar on 21 September 1858, died in Sequim, Washington Territory, on 9 June 1898. [WSP]

DICK, Miss JANET, in Glasgow, a deed, 24 March 1841. [NRS.RD29.3.23]

DICK, JOHN, born 1809, a wool spinner in Bankend, Stablestore, Douglas, at present a prisoner in Glasgow, legal husband of Anne Caldwell, was accused of bigamy with Marion Brown in 1848. [NRS.AD14.48.466]

DICKIE, ADAM, a weaver, was admitted as a burgess and guilds-brother of Glasgow on 28 September 1815. [GBR]

DICKIE, JAMES, a manufacturer from Glasgow, settled in New York by 1801. [NRS.CS17,1.9/63; CS17.1.21/319; CS17.1.18/421]

DICKIE, RICHARD, master of the brigantine Mary Ann of Port Glasgow, testament, 1810, Comm, Glasgow. [NRS]

DICKSON, DAVID, a machine maker in Hutchestown, Glasgow, son of John Dickson in Lockerbie, Dumfries-shire, heir to his grandfather David Dickson, postmaster of Lockerbie in 1839. [NRS.CS237.D9.45]

DICKSON, ISABELLA, a cooper in Airdrie, died 4 September 1862. [NRS.S/H.1863]

DICKSON, JOHN, born 1830, a blacksmith in Lanarkshire, landed in Hobart, Tasmania, Australia, aboard the Donald McKay on 6 September 1855. [SRA.TD292]

DINNIN, PETER, in 29 Back Wynd, Glasgow, a former soldier of the 1st Regiment of Foot, with his wife and five children, applied to settle in Canada on 2 April 1827. [TNA.CO384.5.823]

DIXON, HENRY, baptised on 10 March 1785 in Gorbals, Glasgow, son of William Dixon and his wife Janet Smith, died in Cove Valley, Hanover, Jamaica, in 1801. [AJ.2779][GM.71.371]

DIXON, JAMES, born 1796 in Lanarkshire, emigrated via Port Glasgow to New York in 1827, naturalised in D.C. on 4 January 1839. [DC. Circuit Court]

DIXON, WILLIAM, in Glasgow, a sub-tack. 22 February 1841. [NRS.RD29.3.23]

DIXON, Captain, master of the Admiral of Glasgow bound from Stornaway with passengers to Quebec in 1851. [BPP]

DOBIE, DAVID, died at Gartferry House, Lanarkshire, on 11 July 1836. [Weekly Chronicle, 9.9.1836]

DOBBIE, JAMES, a weaver from Glasgow, and his family, settled in Lanark, Upper Canada, by 1826. [BPP.2.166]

DOBIE, JAMES, born 1806, eldest son of the late David Dobie of Gartferry, died in Fredericton, New Brunswick, on 8 December 1839. [New Brunswick Courier, 14.12.1839]

DOBBIE, JOHNSTON, a sailor in London, son and heir of William Dobbie in Glasgow, in 1793. [NRS.S/H]

DOBIE, ROBERT, born 1843, son of Thomas Dobie and his wife Martha Harrower, died in Australia on 7 May 1863. [Lanark gravestone]

DOBBIE, THOMAS, of the Cambuslang Emigration Society, with his wife and family, emigrated via Greenock aboard the George Canning, Captain Potter, bound for Quebec on 14 April 1821. [TNA.CO42.189] 43

DOBIE, W. H., from Glasgow, married Ann Elleison McDowal, daughter of A. McDowal late of Two Mile Wood, Jamaica, at Collean Cottage, Ayrshire, on 2 August 1842. [NBC.10.9.1842]

DOCHERTY, SAMUEL, born 6 June 1838 in Glasgow, studied at the Ratisbon Seminary, Germany, in 1852, and in Dublin, Ireland, in 1862, died in San Francisco, California. [SIG.296] [RSC.258]

DONALD, COLIN DUNLOP, born 1777, a writer in Glasgow, died 18 September 1859, husband of Marianne Stirling, born 1786, died 4 March 1826. [Ramshorn church]

FLEMING, DAVID, born 1782, son of John Fleming in Glasgow, was educated at Glasgow University in 1795, a merchant who died in Charleston, South Carolina, on 31 August 1809. [MAGU]

FLEMING, JAMES, born 1803, in Muirside, died 28 December 1855, husband of Jane Allison, born 1809, died 8 September 1896. [Carmunnock gravestone]

FLEMING, JOHN STUART, in Nelson, New Zealand, son and heir of Andrew Fleming, a weaving agent in Strathaven, who died on 14 February 1850; also, heir to his aunt Jean Fleming, widow of Thomas Reid, a manufacturer in Glasgow, who died on 16 October 1880. [NRS.S/H]

FLEMMING, WILLIAM, of the Strathaven and Kilbride Emigration Society, with his wife and family, emigrated via Greenock aboard the George Canning, Captain Potter, bound for Quebec on 14 April 1821. [TNA.CO42.189]

FLEMING, WILLIAM, of Sawmillfield, born 1808, an accountant in Glasgow, died 1864. [Ramshorn church]

FLEMING, WILLIAM, born 15 February 1842, eldest son of James Fleming and his wife Isabella McLaren in Glasgow, a coppersmith who died in St Andrew's, Jamaica, on 3 September 1862. [Hampden gravestone, Jamaica]

FLOOD, JOHN, a farmer and weaver in Anderston, applied to settle in Canada on 4 March 1815. [NRS.RH9] [TNA.CO385.2]

FORD, WILLIAM, a merchant from Glasgow, in Boston, Massachusetts in 1819. [NRS.CS17.1.38/267]

FORREST, ALEXANDER, born 1823, a bricklayer from Glasgow, emigrated to South Australia, in 1849. [BPP.11.208]

FORREST, ANDREW, born 1832, son of Robert Forrest, died in New Zealand in 1879. [Carluke gravestone]

FORREST, ANNIE, born 1827, a spinster from Glasgow, emigrated to South Australia, in 1849. [BPP.11.208]

FORREST, JAMES, born 1826, a farm servant from Glasgow, emigrated to South Australia, in 1849. [BPP.11.208]

FORREST, JANE, born 1832, a spinster from Glasgow, emigrated to South Australia, in 1849. [BPP.11.208]

FORREST, MARY, born 1839, daughter of Robert Forrest, died in New Orleans, Louisiana, in 1853. [Carluke gravestone]

FORREST, THOMAS, born 1830, a farm servant from Glasgow, emigrated to South Australia, in 1849. [BPP.11.208]

FORREST, THOMAS, born 1851, son of Robert Forrest, died in New Zealand in 1879. [Carluke gravestone]

FORREST, WILLIAM, born 1847, son of Robert Forrest, died in Melbourne, Victoria, Australia, in 1875. [Carluke gravestone]

FORRESTER, WALTER, only son of Somerville Forrester a merchant in Jamaica, matriculated at Glasgow University in 1817. [MAGU]

FOSTER, MARGARET, only daughter of James Foster in Carnegie Park, Glasgow, married John King of Sherwood Park, Tobago, at Carnegie Park on 7 June 1819. [BM.5.505]

FOSTER Captain PATRICK, son of James Foster of Carnegie Park, Port Glasgow, died on the coast of Sumatra on 7 April 1822. [SM.90.631]

FOSTER, RALPH, in Drummoyne, died in February 1810. [NRS.S/H.1853]

FOWLER, MARGARET, wife of John Walker in Montreal, Quebec, son and heir of Rebecca Muir, wife of Thomas Fowler in Glasgow, who died on 6 November 1835. [NRS.S/H]

FOWLIS, ALLAN, son of Allan Fowlis a wood-merchant in Glasgow, died at Cape Henry, St Domingo on 10 July 1821. [S.5.224]

FOWLIS, GEORGE, born 1797, son of Allan Fowlis, a wood-merchant in Glasgow, died at Cape Henry, St Domingo on 10 July 1820, testament, 25 August 1824. [NRS.CC8.8.150] [S.5.224]

FRAME, ANDREW, born 1795, a merchant from Glasgow, emigrated via Greenock aboard the William of New York bound for N.Y. on 4

September 1817, landed there on 17 October 1817. [NY Municipal Archives] [NY Commercial Advertiser, 18.10.1817]

FRAME, JOHN, formerly a calico printer in Glasgow, died in Nottawasaga, Upper Canada, on 15 September 1844. [SG.1342]

FRAME, NINIAN, of the Glasgow Wrights Emigration Society, with his wife and family, emigrated via Greenock aboard the George Canning, Captain Potter, bound for Quebec on 14 April 1821. [TNA.CO42.189]

FRASER, ANDREW STRANG, a merchant, son of John Strang a sugar sampler in the Exchange, Glasgow, was admitted as a burgess and guilds-brother of Glasgow, on 13 April 1841. [GBR]

FRASER, EWAN, a merchant in Demerara, a partner of the firm Campbell, Fraser, and Company in Glasgow, appointed his partner Colin Campbell, a merchant in Glasgow, as his attorney, deed was subscribed in Demerara on 20 June 1814. [NRS.RD5.64.248]

FRASER, H., born 1840, possibly from Glasgow, a volunteer under Garibaldi in Italy during 1860. [SHR.57.175]

FRASER, JAMES, a skipper in Port Glasgow, testament, 1820, Comm. Glasgow. [NRS]

FRASER, Dr JOHN, eldest son of James Fraser in Glasgow, died in Kingston, Jamaica, in 1794. [GM.64.768]

FRASER, JOHN, born 13 May 1789, second son of Reverend J. Fraser in Libberton, Lanarkshire, died in Jamaica on 15 November 1821. [BM.11.382][F.I.255][EEC.17262][DPCA]

FRASER, JOHN, a merchant in St John's in the West Indies, grandson and heir of John McGregor a japanner in Glasgow, who died 5 January 1832. [NRS.S/H]

FRAZER, JOHN, a cloth merchant from Glasgow, was admitted as a burgess and freeman of Ayr on 4 March 1829. [ABR]

FRASER, J., a schoolmaster in Carluke, father of Hugh Forsyth Fraser who died in Tijuca, Rio de Janeiro, Brazil, on 16 February 1869. [S.8005]

FRASER, ROBERT, with family of six, members of the Lesmahagow Emigration Society in Lanark, bound for Quebec in 1820. [TNA.CO384.6.101062]

FRASER, PAUL, in Glasgow, applied to settle in Canada on 4 March 1815. [NRS.RH9]

FRASER, WILLIAM, a planter in Virginia, nephew and heir of Daniel Fraser in the Gorbals, Glasgow, 1826. [NRS.S/H]

FREEBAIRN, JOHN, a mason, vintner and former baillie of Rutherglen, was accused of celebrating clandestine marriages in 1823. [NRS.AD.14.23.59]

FREEBAIRN, MARGARET MAXWELL, in Hamilton, daughter and heir of Charles Freebairn a wright in Jamaica, later in Hamilton, who died in January 1791. [NRS.S/H]

FREEBAIRN, MARY, in Hamilton, daughter and heir of Charles Freebairn a wright in Jamaica, later in Hamilton, who died in January 1791. [NRS.S/H]

FREELAND, THOMAS, born 1793, son of John Freeland in Glasgow, was educated at Glasgow University in 1806, died at Aux Cayes, Haiti, on 17 November 1822. [MAGU]

FRENCH, ANNE, widow of James Todd in New York, and niece of Dr Witherspoon of Princeton College, died in Villafield, Glasgow, on 16 July 1840. [W.54]

FRENCH, WILLIAM, a clerk at the Verreville Glassworks in Glasgow, settled in New York before December 1809. [NRS.CS17.1.29/108]

FULLARTON, JAMES, a ships carpenter in St John, New Brunswick, heir to Daniel McNaught a minister in Biggar, 1820. [NRS.S/H]

FULLARTON, WILLIAM, born 1802, formerly a bookseller and publisher in Glasgow, died in Funchal, Madeira, on 4 March 1844, was buried in the British Cemetery there. [ARM]; inventory, 1846. [NRS]

FYFE, ARCHIBALD, a marble cutter in Glasgow, died in 1794. [NRS.CS96.4337]

GALBRAITH, ALEXANDER, of the Glasgow Canadian Emigration Society, with his wife and family, emigrated via Greenock aboard the George Canning, Captain Potter, bound for Quebec on 14 April 1821. [TNA.CO42.189]

GALBRAITH, DAVID, born 1770, son of John Galbraith a tenant farmer in Anniston, Symington, and his wife Janet Galloway, a surgeon who died in Jamaica on 13 October 1793. [Symington gravestone]

GALBRAITH, JAMES, from Glasgow, a tinsmith in New York, heir to his parents James Galbraith, a tinsmith in Glasgow, and his wife Mary Smith, 1843. [NRS.S/H]

GALBRAITH, WILLIAM, with one dependent, members of the Lesmahagow Emigration Society in Lanark, bound for Quebec in 1820. [TNA.CO384.6.101062]

GALLOWAY, ALEXANDER, agent for the Western Bank of Scotland in Airdrie, 1849. [POD]

GALLOWAY, ROBERT, son of Andrew Galloway a merchant in Glasgow, died in Fredericksburg, Virginia, on 1 August 1794. [EA.3212]

GALT, JOHN, a tailor at Jack and Paterson in Trongate, Glasgow, was admitted as a burgess and guilds-brother of Glasgow on 16 April 1840, having served an apprenticeship with Cleland and Jack, upholsterers, burgesses and guild-brothers. [GBR]

GAMBLE, WILLIAM, from Glasgow, emigrated via Ireland to America in 1800, settled in Ohio. [BLG]

GARDEN, MARY ROBERTSON, born 1816, second daughter of Alexander Garden in Glasgow, died in Rome on 18 November 1834. [Rome Protestant Cemetery gravestone]

GARDINER, DAVID, from Glasgow, died in Lisbon, Portugal, in 1812. [SM.74.520]

GARDINER, MATTHEW, born 18 August 1776 in Glasgow, son of James Gardiner, graduated MA from Glasgow University in 1793 and DD in 1831, minister at Bothwell from 1802 until his death on 4 June 1865. [F.3.232]

GARDINER, ROBERT, of the Hamilton Emigration Society, with a son and daughter, emigrated via Greenock on board the Commerce of Greenock, Captain Coverdale, bound for Quebec on 11 May 1821, was granted land in Dalhousie, Upper Canada, on 15 July 1821. [TNA.CO42.89] [PAO]

GARDNER, JAMES CORBET, eldest son of James Gardner a perfumer in Glasgow, died in Mobile, Alabama, on 19 June 1844. [SG.1324]

GARDNER, WALTER, President of the Wishaw Emigration Society with his wife and family, emigrated via Greenock aboard the David of London, master David Gemmill, bound for Quebec on 19 May 1821. [TNA.CO42.189]

GARRICK, GEORGE, born 1809, Glasgow city architect and master of works, died 2 May 1890. [Ramshorn church]

GARROWAY, ROBERT, a merchant of Garroway and Hope acid manufacturers, was admitted as a burgess and guilds-brother of Glasgow on 9 March 1841, as eldest son of Iver John Garroway, a merchant, burgess and guilds-brother. [GBR]

GAVIN, JAMES, first son of William Gavin a merchant in Jamaica, matriculated at Glasgow University in 1811. [MAGU]

GELLATLY, Captain, of the Rebecca of Glasgow, from the River Clyde to Quebec and Montreal in 1835-1836. [QM]

GEMMEL, JOHN, a mason from the Gorbals, Glasgow, settled in Lanark, Upper Canada, in 1820. [NRS.NRAS.0396] [GA.TD293.1.5]

GEMMILL, JOHN, of the Glasgow Trongate Emigration Society, with his wife and family, emigrated via Greenock aboard the David of London, master David Gemmil, bound for Quebec on 19 May 1821. [TNA.CO42.189]

GEMMILL, JOHN, of the Glasgow Trongate Emigration Society, emigrated via Greenock aboard the David of London bound for Quebec on 19 May 1821.[TNA.CO42.189]

GEMMILL, SAMUEL, of the Rutherglen Emigration Society, emigrated via Greenock aboard the Commerce of Greenock, Captain Covendale, bound for Quebec on 11 May 1821, was granted land in Lanark, Upper Canada, on 6 August 1821. [TNA.CO42.189] [PAO]

GEMMELL, THOMAS, and his wife, from Glasgow, emigrated via Greenock aboard the Portaferry, bound for Quebec in May 1832. [QM.13.6.1832] [GWS]

GENTLES, GEORGE, jr, messenger at arms, Airdrie, 1849. [POD]

GERARD, JOHN, youngest son of Lieutenant Colonel Gerard of Rochsoles, Lanarkshire, died in Graz, Austria, on 31 December 1858. [W.XX.2051]

GIBB, GEORGE S., born 1796 in Glasgow, died in Madeira on 14 March 1823. [ARM]

GIBB, JAMES, son of John Gibb [1760-1802] farmer at Hillhead, Carluke, and his wife Agnes Watson [1765-1845], emigrated to Quebec before 1825, died 1833 in Quebec, father of James Lawson Gibb. [Carluke gravestone]

GIBB, JOHN, son of John Gibb [1760-1802] farmer at Hillhead, Carluke, and Jean Lawson [1756-1839], emigrated to Quebec or Montreal before 1826. [Carluke gravestone]

GIBB, JOHN GEORGE, born 1837, son of Elias Gibb in Glasgow, died on 25 July 1855, buried in the British Cemetery, Funchal, Madeira. [ARM]

GIBB, SARAH, daughter of Thomas Gibb in Millwood, married John Wedderspoon, a merchant in San Francisco, California, there on 7 June 1859. [CM.21792]

GIBB, THOMAS, son of John Gibb [1760-1802] farmer at Hillhead, Carluke and Jean Lawson [1756-1839], emigrated to Quebec before 1826. [Carluke gravestone]

GIBSON, ARCHIBALD, a shoemaker in Meikle Govan, was admitted as a burgess and guilds-brother of Glasgow on 31 March 1803, as younger son of John Gibson, in Meikle Govan, a cordiner, burgess and guilds-brother. [GBR]

GIBSON, DANIEL, in Munro, Louisiana, son and heir of Jean Henderson Gibson, wife of Hugh McCallum a weaver in Glasgow, who died 4 July 1849. [NRS.S/H]

GIBSON, JAMES, [1773-1831], and his wife Janet Glasgow, [1797-1872], were parents of John Gibson who died in Keerang, Australia, on 1 March 1879. [Carstairs gravestone]

GIBSON, JANET, wife of John Brown, in Montreal, Quebec, daughter and heir to James Brown a farmer in Overburn, who died 6 February 1842, also, sister and heir of William Gibson a farmer in Overburn, Lamington, Biggar, and to her brother Robert Gibson, second son of James Gibson a farmer in Overburn, 1867. [NRS.S/H]

GIBSON, JOHN, of Oakbank, born 1754, a merchant in Glasgow, died 1814. [Ramshorn church]

GIBSON, JOHN, schoolmaster at Lamington, trial papers, 1795. [NRS.JC26.1795.30]

GIBSON, PETER, a planter in Trelawney, Cornwall County, Jamaica, appointed John Gordon, Charles Stirling and James Fyffe, merchants in Glasgow, as his attornies, 25 April 1818. [NRS.RD5.150.4]

GIBSON, THOMAS, a skipper in Port Glasgow, testament, 1805, Comm. Glasgow. [NRS]

GIBSON, THOMAS, a carter in Redmyre, Cambusnethan, was accused of the culpable homicide of Charles Forrest in Stewart Street, Carluke, in 1847. [NRS.AD14.47.288]

GILCHRIST, ALEXANDER, a skipper in Glasgow, testament, 1823, Comm. Glasgow. [NRS]

GILCHRIST, JAMES, a mason in Strathaven, his wife Agnes Mitchell, and their daughter Agnes Gilchrist, Letters of Suspension, in 1736. [NRS.GD1.221.29]

GILCHRIST, JAMES, agent of the British Linen Company in Wishaw in 1849. [POD]

GILFILLAN, THOMAS, a mariner in Port Glasgow, testament, 1819, Comm. Glasgow. [NRS]

GILKISON, DAVID, agent of the Clydesdale Bank in Port Glasgow in 1849. [POD]

GILKISON, WILLIAM, from Glasgow, died in Tuscarora, Upper Canada, on 25 April 1833. [SG.146]

GILLESPIE, ALEXANDER, in Toronto, Ontario, son of George Gillespie in Biggar Park, Lanarkshire, married Maria Holmes, second daughter of Colonel Patterson of the Royal Artillery, in Woolwich, Upper Canada, on 26 December 1843. [AJ.5017][EEC.21001][W.5.439]

GILLESPIE, DAVID, a boy found guilty of street robbery, was sentenced in Glasgow to fourteen years transportation in 1815. [NRS.GD1.959]

GILLESPIE, JAMES, son of George Gillespie of Biggar Park, died in Canada on 27 July 1832. [AJ.4422]

GILLESPIE, JAMES ROBERT, born 1833, son of Robert Gillespie, MD, died in Ipswich, Queensland, Australia, on 27 February 1866. [Biggar gravestone]

GILLESPIE, THOMAS, born 1765 in Wiston, Lanarkshire, died in Jamaica on 29 April 1799. [Wiston gravestone]

GILMOUR, ALLAN, of the Glasgow Trongate Emigration Society, with his wife and family, emigrated via Greenock aboard the David of London, master David Gemmil, bound for Quebec on 19 May 1821. [TNA.CO42.189]

GILMOUR, HUGH, of the Glasgow Trongate Emigration Society, with his wife and family, emigrated via Greenock aboard the David of London, master David Gemmil, bound for Quebec on 19 May 1821. [TNA.CO42.189]

GILMOUR, JAMES, President of the Lanarkshire Emigration Society, with his wife, two sons and two daughters, emigrated to Canada on the Earl of Buckinghamshire, Captain Johnston, in 29 April 1821, settled in Sherbrook, Upper Canada, on 31 July 1821. [PAO][TNA.CO42.189]

GILMOUR, JAMES, of the Glasgow Trongate Emigration Society, with his wife, emigrated via Greenock aboard the David of London, master David Gemmil, bound for Quebec on 19 May 1821. [TNA.CO42.189]

GILMOUR, JAMES, in Ozark, Missouri, brother and heir of Mary Gillies in Glasgow who died 28 December 1866. [NRS.S/H]

GILMOUR, JOHN MORTON, eldest son of Robert Gilmour, a merchant from Glasgow, later in Lancaster, Virginia, 1799, 1800. [NRS.NRAS.O623.TMJ. 427/68; CS17.1.18/138]

GILMOUR, JOHN, of the Glasgow Trongate Emigration Society, with his wife, emigrated via Greenock aboard the David of London, master David Gemmil, bound for Quebec on 19 May 1821. [TNA.CO42.189] 52

GILMOUR, JOHN, born 1738, a mason in Carmunnock, died in 1834. [Carmunnock gravestone]

GILMOUR, JOHN K., only son of Matthew Gilmour in Glasgow, died in Newhaven, Connecticut, on 17 December 1849. [W.1079]

GILMOUR, WILLIAM, of the Lanarkshire Emigration Society, emigrated to Canada on the Earl of Buckinghamshire, Captain Johnston, on 29 April 1821, settled in Sherbrook, Upper Canada, on 31 July 1821. [PAO][TNA.CO42.189]

GIRDWOOD, JOHN, late builder in Kirkintilloch, son of George Girdwood in Carnwath, died in Hamilton, Canada West, on 10 December 1856. [EEC.20990]

GLASGOW, MARY, daughter of John Glasgow a merchant in Glasgow, married Charles Foote, MD, of Gibraltar, there on 19 December 1823. [SM.93.127]

GLASSFORD, HENRY, of Dougaldston, was admitted as a burgess and guilds-brother of Glasgow on 6 October 1795, as eldest son of John Glassford a merchant, burgess and guilds-brother. [GBR]

GLASSFORD, MATTHEW, a merchant of Young, Glassford, and Company, calico printers, was admitted as a burgess and guilds-brother of Glasgow on 4 July 1840. [GBR]

GLEN, CATHERINE, born 1754, widow of William Kidston formerly in Halifax, New Brunswick, died in Anderston on 11 December 1838. [Acadian Recorder, 2.3.1839]

GLEN, DAVID CORSE, an engineer in Glasgow, brother and heir of James Glen a merchant in San Francisco, California, who died in January 1856. [NRS.S/H]

GLEN, ROBERT, with family of four members of the Lesmahagow Emigration Society in Lanark, bound for Quebec in 1820. [TNA.CO384.6.101062]

GOODWIN, ALEXANDER, of the Bridgeton Transatlantic Emigration Society, with his wife and family, emigrated via Greenock aboard the George Canning, Captain Potter, bound for Quebec on 14 April 1821. [TNA.CO42.189]

GORDON, HAMILTON, son of Colonel Gordon of Harperfield, Lanarkshire, a Captain of the 42d Highlanders, died in Cairo, Egypt, on 23 June 1851. [W.1247]

GORDON, JEAN, wife of John Livingstone a collier in Bellahouston, Glasgow, daughter and heir to her father James Gordon a smith in Jamaica, 1799. [NRS.S/H]

GORDON, PETER, son of James Gordon a merchant in Glasgow, was educated at Glasgow University in 1822, a divinity student in 1826, a minister of the Secession Church in America. [MAGU][AUPC]

GORDON, ROBERT, a merchant in Virginia, in Glasgow, a sasine in 1823. [NRS.RS54.159]

GOULD, WILLIAM, from Glasgow, a Lieutenant of the 5th West Indian Regiment, died in Belize on 11 May 1801. [GM.72.181]

GOURLIE, ROBERT, from Motherwell, Lanarkshire, a watchmaker in Maiden Lane, New York, from 1803. [ANY]

GOVAN, JEAN, wife of John Paton in Hamilton, sister and heir of James Govan a wright in Jamaica, 1789. [NRS.S/H]

GOURLAY, WILLIAM, of the Cambuslang Emigration Society, with his wife and family, emigrated via Greenock aboard the George Canning, Captain Potter, bound for Quebec on 14 April 1821. [TNA.CO42.189]

GOW, ANDREW, from Georgia, a merchant in Charleston, South Carolina, in 1798. [VMHB.6.135]

GOWANS, JAMES, born 1766 in Lanarkshire, emigrated to USA in 1821, lived in Indiana, Ohio, and Kentucky, died in Louisville, Kentucky, on 22 October 1849. [SG.18.1877]

GOWANS, WILLIAM, born 29 March 1803 in Lesmahagow, emigrated to America in 1821, a book dealer and author in Philadelphia, Pennsylvania, moved to New York in 1828, died there on 27 November 1870. [WA]

GRAEME, CAMERON, in Glasgow, applied to settle in Canada on 25 February 1815. [NRS.RH9]

GRAHAM, ALEXANDER, born 1763, a physician in Glasgow, emigrated via Ireland aboard the Eagle bound for New York on 27 August 1803. [BM]

GRAHAM, ALEXANDER, of the Rutherglen Emigration Society, with his wife, two sons, and two daughters, emigrated via Greenock aboard the Commerce of Greenock, Captain Covendale, bound for Quebec on 11 May 1821, was granted land in Lanark, Upper Canada, on 10 May 1821. [TNA.CO42.189] [PAO]

GRAHAM, ALEXANDER, of the St John's Parish Emigration Society, with his wife, two sons, and two daughters, emigrated via Greenock aboard the Commerce of Greenock, Captain Covendale, bound for Quebec on 11 May 1821, was granted land in Dalhousie, Upper Canada, on 10 July 1821. [TNA.CO42.189] [PAO]

GRAHAM, ALEXANDER, a merchant at the Islay Distillery cellars, Wellington Court, 22 Argyll Street, Glasgow, was admitted as a burgess and guilds-brother of Glasgow on 20 November 1823 as son of William Graham a coppersmith, burgess and guilds-brother. [GBR]

GRAHAM, ALEXANDER, probably from Glasgow, emigrated via Liverpool aboard the New York bound for New York in 1826, a merchant in New York. [ANY]

GRAHAM, ANDREW, born 1769, a physician in Glasgow, emigrated via Ireland to New York on the Eagle of New York on 27 August 1803. [BM.ms]

GRAHAM, DANIEL, a shipmaster in Glasgow, in 1793. [NRS.S/H]

GRAHAM, DUNCAN, a sailor in Glasgow, in 1793. [NRS.S/H]

GRAHAM, GEORGE, a merchant in Copenhagen, Denmark, later a planter in St Croix, Danish West Indies, died in Glasgow on 12 June 1798, probate 1800, PCC. [TNA] [HCR.213] [AJ.2630]

GRAHAM, JAMES, a merchant in Glasgow, late partner in the firm of Graham and Neilson, died in Trinidad, testament, 1806, Comm. Glasgow. [NRS]

GRAHAM, JAMES, fourth son of Robert Burdon Graham of Feddel, was educated at Glasgow University around 1788, died in Jamaica on 16 January 1806. [Car.4.17]

GRAHAM, JAMES, born 1795, son of James Graham of Leuinsdale, [1769-1856], and his wife Helen Steele, [1766-1860], died at Oak Creek, Wisconsin, on 28 September 1851. [Lesmahagow gravestone]

GRAHAM, JAMES, of Ballewan, a merchant and manufacturer in Glasgow, [1776-1842], and his wife Margaret Paterson, [1775-1830], parents of Henry Graham, born 1809, a writer who died in Madeira on 17 April 1848 and was buried in the British Cemetery in Funchal. [ARM] [Ramshorn gravestone, Glasgow]

GRAHAM, JOHN, of the Bridgeton Transatlantic Emigration Society, with his wife and family, emigrated via Greenock aboard the George Canning, Captain Potter, bound for Quebec on 14 April 1821. [TNA.CO42.189]

GRAHAM, JOHN, in Kittochside, heir to his grand-uncle David McCulloch a surgeon in Jamaica, 1851. [NRS.S/H]

GRAHAM, MATTHEW, born 10 August 1811, son of Matthew Graham minister at Calton, Glasgow, was educated at Glasgow University, minister at Baillieston from 1844 until 28 January 1856, died in Glasgow on 4 June 1856. [F.3.226]

GRAHAM, ROBERT CUNNINGHAME, second son of Nicholas Graham of Gartmore, matriculated at Glasgow University in 1748, later a planter and Receiver General of Jamaica, died at Gartmore on 11 December 1797. [MAGU] [NRS.GD22.1.566]

GRAHAM, ROBERT, born 1782, son of Walter Graham in Port Glasgow, died on Sullivan's Island near Charleston, South Carolina, in 1802. [AJ.2852]

GRAHAM, ROBERT, tenth son of John Graham formerly a merchant in Jamaica, matriculated at Glasgow University in 1816. [MAGU]

GRAHAM, W., of Philadelphia, Pennsylvania, later of Glasgow in 1811. [NRS.CS17.1.31/191]

GRAHAM, WILLIAM, a merchant of William Graham and Company, grocers at 54 Gallowgate, Glasgow, was admitted as a burgess and guilds-brother of Glasgow on 13 September 1817. [GBR]

GRAHAM, WILLIAM, of the North Albion Emigration Society, emigrated via Greenock on board the Commerce of Greenock, Captain Coverdale, bound for Quebec on 1 May 1821. [TNA.CO42.89]

GRAHAM, WILLIAM LECKIE, second son of John Graham formerly a merchant in Jamaica, matriculated at Glasgow University in 1817, a merchant in Glasgow, died in St Thomas, Danish West Indies, on 16 June 1843. [EEC.20635][MAGU]

GRANT, Mrs ANNE MCVICAR, born 1755 in Glasgow, an American author, died in 1838. [SSA]

GRANT, JAMES COLQUHOUN, in Hanover, Jamaica, his executors there appointed James Jackson McLachlan in Glasgow as their factor on 11 May 1820. [NRS.RD5.282.690]

GRANT, JOHN, in Glasgow, a deed, registered 14 April 1841. [NRS.RD29.3.23]

GRANT, JOHN, born 1834, a boilersmith from Lanarkshire, landed in Hobart, Tasmania, Australia, from the Donald McKay on 6 September 1855. [SRA.TD292]

GRANT, JOHN, second son of Duncan Grant of Newhall House, married Olga Matilda Alexandrina, baroness of Wegner, in Weimar, Germany, on 23 November 1848. [EEC.21744]

GRANT, ROBERT, President of the St John's Parish Emigration Society, with his wife and three sons, emigrated via Greenock aboard the Commerce of Greenock, Captain Covendale, bound for Quebec on 11 May 1821, was granted land in Ramsay, Upper Canada, on 1 August 1821. [TNA.CO42.189] [PAO]

GRAY, CATHERINE, daughter of George Gray, farmer of Newbigging Mill, Carnwath, a declarator of marriage, versus Andrew Belches, a banker in Glasgow, in 1820. [NRS.CC8.6.1784]

GRAY, GEORGE, in Glasgow, father of Isabella Gray, born 1820, and Jane Gray born 1823, both servants, who both emigrated to South Australia in 1848. [BPP.11.338],

GRAY, GEORGE, born 1822, a garden master in Glasgow, with Jane Gray born 1824, and Isabella born 1821, emigrated to South Australia, in 1849. [BPP.11.189]

GRAY, JOHN, born in Glasgow, lately from Charleston, South Carolina, died on 23 July 1803. [Bahamas Royal Gazette, 24.7.1804]

GRAY, JOHN, was found guilty of reset n Glasgow, and was sentenced to transportation to the colonies for 7 years on29 April 1812. [SM.84.394]

GRAY, MARGARET, born 1767, wife of Robert Watson from Lanark, died in Montreal, Quebec, on 16 August 1832. [GA.4270]

GRAY, WILLIAM, from Glasgow, settled in Virginia by 1796. [NRS.CS17.1]

GRAY, WILLIAM, born 1780 in Glasgow, a merchant in Charleston, South Carolina, was naturalised on 23 October 1813. [NARA.M1183.1]

GRAY, WILLIAM, a boy, guilty of stealing a watch, was sentenced in Glasgow to seven years transportation to the colonies in 1815. [NRS.GD1.959]

GRAY, WILLIAM, a merchant, was admitted as a burgess and guildsbrother of Glasgow on 15 May 1817, by right of his wife Mary Hutcheson, daughter of James Hutcheson a burgess and guilds-brother. [GBR]

GRAY, ..., agent in Lanark for the Western Bank of Scotland in 1849. [POD]

GREEN, JAMES S., born 1850, from Glasgow, died 11 March 1846, buried in the British Cemetery in Funchal, Madeira. [ARM]

GREENHORN, Captain, of the Favourite of Port Glasgow from the River Clyde with passengers to Montreal and Quebec in 1843, 1847. [GA]

GREENLAW, JANET, wife of David Black a merchant in Nova Scotia, daughter and heir of John Greenlaw a merchant in Glasgow, 1789. [NRS.S/H]

GREGORIE, JAMES, a merchant from Glasgow, was naturalised in South Carolina on 19 October 1803. [NARA.M1183.1]

GREGORY, RICHARD FRANCIS, a tailor of the Lace and Corset Warehouse, 19 Hutcheson Street, Glasgow, was admitted as a burgess and guilds-brother of Glasgow on 5 September 1828. [GBR]

GRIERSON, PHILIP, a merchant in Glasgow, was admitted as a burgess and freeman of Ayr on 14 November 1810. [ABR]

GRINDLAY, JOHN, an attorney in Charleston, South Carolina, probate 10 October 1806 in Glasgow. [NRS]

GULLAN, JOHN G., formerly a teacher in Glasgow, died in Montreal, Quebec, on 12 January 1845. [W.545]

GULLAN, MARGARET, wife of Hugh Cameron from Glasgow, died in Hamilton, Canada West, on 1 September 1849. [SG.1866]

GUNN, CRAWFORD, of the Glasgow Canadian Emigration Society, with his wife, emigrated via Greenock aboard the George Canning, Captain Potter, bound for Quebec on 14 April 1821. [TNA.CO42.189]

HADDOW, JOHN, born 1769, son of John Haddow, [1725-1803], and Margaret Inglis, [1739-1791], died in Grenada on 11 September 1802. [Lanark gravestone]

HAGGART, ALEXANDER, born 1787, a labourer from Barony, Glasgow, emigrated to New York on the George of New York on 12 August 1807. [TNA.PC1.3790]

HALIBURTON, MARK, born 1765, died 17 January 1842. [Ramshorn gravestone]

HALL, JOHN SHARP, born 1797, son of Reverend James Hall in Lesmahagow, educated at Glasgow University in 1811, a Writer to the Signet in 1821, died in Halifax, Nova Scotia, on 30 September 1885. [MAGU]

HALLEY, EBENEZER, a minister in New York, son and heir of William Halley in Glasgow, who died on 5 August 1854. [NRS.S/H]

HAMILTON, ALEXANDER BROWNLEE, a mason in Strathaven, died 5 August 1866. [NRS.S/H]

HAMILTON, GEORGE WILLIAM, son of John Hamilton of Northbank in Glasgow, and his wife Helen Bogle, a planter in Tulloch, St Thomas in the Vale, Jamaica, before 1829, a deed. [NRS.RD5.398.536]

HAMILTON, JAMES, in Glasgow, formerly a skipper and agent in Honduras, testament, 28 April 1803, Comm. Glasgow. [NRS]

HAMILTON, JAMES, born 1800, son of James Hamilton [1758-1825] a merchant in Biggar, and his wife Agnes Watson [1765-1845], died in Jamaica on 3 January 1824. [St Mary's, Biggar, gravestone]

HAMILTON, JAMES, brother of Robert Hamilton in Dowan, a planter in Dowan, St George's, Jamaica, in 1800. [NRS.NRAS.0620]

HAMILTON, JOHN, of Dowan, a merchant in Glasgow, partner in the firm of Simon Brown and Company, merchants in Glasgow, testaments, 1791, Comm. Glasgow. [NRS]

HAMILTON, JOHN, born 1781, son of John Hamilton a merchant in Glasgow, educated at Glasgow University in 1793, died in Kingston, Jamaica, on 4 November 1801. [Car.4.17] [MAGU] [GM.72.181]

HAMILTON, JOHN, in Jamaica, son and heir of John Hamilton a clock-maker in Glasgow, 1804. [NRS.S/H]

HAMILTON, JOHN, a wright and a wood merchant from Strathaven, in America by 1818. [NRS.CS17.1.38/365]

HAMILTON, JOHN, of the Kirkman Finlay Emigration Society, with his wife, and son, emigrated via Greenock on board the Commerce of Greenock, Captain Coverdale, bound for Quebec on 11 May 1821, was granted land in Lanark, Upper Canada, on 27 July 1821. [TNA.CO42.89] [PAO]

HAMILTON, JOHN BLACKWOOD, late in Montreal, Quebec, died in Hamilton on 9 December 1831. [AJ.4382]

HAMILTON, ROBERT, born 1777 in south Lanarkshire, an agent of the London Missionary Society for 36 years, died at Kurumum Mission Station, South Africa, on 11 July 1851. [W.1274]

HAMILTON, ROBERT, fourth son of John Hamilton an officer of Glasgow, matriculated at Glasgow University in 1801, a merchant in Jamaica, died in London in 1840. [MAGU] [NRS.C22482; RD5.193.513]

HAMILTON, THOMAS, master of the Recovery of Glasgow from Greenock to Halifax, Nova Scotia, in 1820, from Greenock to New Orleans, Louisiana, in 1821 and 1822. [NRS.E504.15.131/138/141]

HAMILTON, WILLIAM, of the Glasgow Trongate Emigration Society, emigrated via Greenock aboard the David of London, master David Gemmil, bound for Quebec on 19 May 1821. [TNA.CO42.189]

HAMILTON, WILLIAM, born 1785 in Lanarkshire, a baker, died on 12 March 1825 in St John, New Brunswick. [New Brunswick Courier, 19.3.1825]

HAMILTON, Mrs, of Dalzell, Lanarkshire, died in Cadiz, Spain, on 24 August 1824. [SM.94.511]

HARDY, JOHN, born 9 June 1840 in Glasgow, was at the Ratisbon Seminary in Germany in 1852. [SIG.296]

HARLEY, WILLIAM, a merchant, was admitted as a burgess and guildsbrother of Glasgow on 16 February 1797. [GBR]

HARLEY, WILLIAM, born 1808, third son of William Harley in Willowbank, Glasgow, died in Campobello Island, near St Andrews, New Brunswick, on 5 July 1834. [NBC.12.7.1834] [SG.275]

HARPER, Reverend ALEXANDER, in Lanark, applied to settle in Canada on 1 March 1815. [NRS.RH9]

HARPER, JAMES, born 1802, son of John Harper a merchant in Glasgow, a minister of the Secession Church, died in Shippenburg, Pennsylvania, on 13 May 1876. [MAGU][AUPC]

HARROWER, JAMES, a merchant in Lanark, papers, 1844-1875. [NRS.GD1.182.16]

HART, ELIAS, a merchant trader from Glasgow, was admitted as a burgess and freeman of Ayr on 19 September 1821. [ABR]

HARTWELL, JOHN, master of the Elizabeth of Port Glasgow from Greenock to Wilmington, North Carolina, in 1790. [NRS.E504.15.56]

HASTIE, ROBERT, a merchant in Glasgow, later in New York, testament, 4 August 1796, Comm. Edinburgh. [NRS] [MAGU]

HAY, ALEXANDER, possibly from Monklands, an engineer in Australia by 1854. [NRS.S/H]

HAY, ROBERT, of the Camlachie Emigration Society, with his family, emigrated via Greenock on board the Commerce of Greenock, Captain Coverdale, bound for Quebec on 11 May 1821. [TNA.CO42.89]

HEARTWELL, JOHN, a shipmaster in Port Glasgow, testament, 1796, Comm. Glasgow. [NRS]

HEATHERINGTON, JAMES, of the Glasgow Union Emigration Society, with his wife and family, emigrated via Greenock aboard the George Canning, Captain Potter, bound for Quebec on 14 April 1821. [TNA.CO42.189]

HENDERSON, ALEXANDER, youngest son of Reverend Richard Henderson in Blantyre, was educated at Glasgow University in 1748, died in Dumfries, Virginia, in January 1816. [SM.78.398]

HENDERSON, ARCHIBALD, born 1730, a merchant, died 12 July 1803. [Ramshorn gravestone]

HENDERSON, J., in the Gorbals, applied to settle in Canada in March 1815. [NRS.RH9]

HENDERSON, J. B., son of John Henderson a surgeon in Port Glasgow, died in Jamaica on 16 April 1821. [GrAd.31.8.1821]

HENDERSON, JAMES, son of Archibald Henderson in Glasgow, died in Manchester, Virginia, on 28 December 1799. [AJ.2719]

HENDERSON, JOHN, with his wife, of the Camlachie Emigration Society, emigrated via Greenock on board the Commerce of Greenock, Captain Coverdale, bound for Quebec on 11 May 1821, was granted land in Ramsay, Upper Canada, on 1 August 1821. [TNA.CO42.89] [PAO]

HENDERSON, RICHARD, son of Reverend Henderson in Blantyre, died in Springhill, Georgetown, Maryland, on 29 August 1802. [EA]

HENDERSON, RICHARD, a merchant, was admitted as a burgess and guilds-brother of Glasgow on 4 October 1804, as eldest son of Archibald Henderson a merchant burgess and guilds-brother. [GBR]

HENDERSON, ROBERT, a weaver in Hamilton, son and heir of Anna Perrie, wife of J. Henderson a mason in New York, 1824. [NRS.S/H]

HENDERSON, WILLIAM, of the Rutherglen Emigration Society, with his family, emigrated via Greenock aboard the Commerce of Greenock, Captain Covendale, bound for Quebec on 11 May 1821. [TNA.CO42.189]

HENDERSON, WILLIAM, son of William Henderson, [1802-1875], and his wife Elizabeth Thomson, [1797-1869], died in Melbourne, Victoria, Australia, aged 48. [Covington gravestone]

HENDRICK, JAMES, of the Bridgeton Canadian Emigration Society, with his wife and family, emigrated via Greenock aboard the George Canning, bound for Quebec on 14 April 1821. [TNA.CO42.189]

HENIE, WILLIAM, born 1784 in Glasgow, a mariner who died in Savanna, Georgia, on 11 July 1808. [Savanna Death Register]

HERON, WILLIAM, in Glasgow, applied to settle in Canada on 25 February 1815. [NRS.RH9]

HENRY, ALEXANDER, a merchant in Kingston, Jamaica, co-owner of Glasgow registered ships in 1794. [NRS.CE60.11.3; 6/69/106]

HEUGH, JOHN, born 1815, son of Reverend Hugh Heugh in Glasgow, was educated at Glasgow University in 1830, died in d'Aquila, Italy, on 14 August 1893. [SGS]

HEYNS, JAMES, born 1778 in Lanark, a mariner who naturalised in Charleston, South Carolina, on 23 August 1813. [NARA.M1183.1]

HEYWOOD, JOSHUA, born 1758, died in January 1828, husband of Bridget Collins, born 1758, died 27 May 1848, parents of Margaret Heywood, born 1804, died in October 1830. [Ramshorn church]

HILL, ANDREW, President of the Govan Emigration Society, with his wife, three sons, and two daughters, emigrated via Greenock on board the Commerce of Greenock, Captain Coverdale, bound for Quebec on 11 May 1821, was granted land in Dalhousie, Upper Canada, on 25 July 1821. [TNA.CO42.89] [PAO]

HILL, ROBERT, a merchant from Glasgow, was admitted as a burgess and guilds-brother of Glasgow, on 20 June 1801, died in Trinidad on 8 January 1820. [GBR][EA.5874.167] [AJ.3767]

HILL, ROBERT, a writer in Edinburgh, son of James Hill a writer in Glasgow, was admitted as a Notary Public on 1 March 1792, died 12 February 1843. [NRS.NP2.34.323]

HINCKSMAN, RICHARD, a merchant from Glasgow, died in Jamaica in June 1797. [EEC.12365] [GM.67.711]

HIND, JOSEPH, born 1785, a labourer in Port Glasgow, emigrated via there aboard the Favourite of St John bound for St John, New Brunswick, on 22 October 1815. [PANB.ms.RS23E.19798]

HISLOP, LAWRENCE, jr., born 1811, eldest son of John Hislop in Biggar, died on Leogan Estate, Montego Bay, Jamaica, on 16 April 1839. [SG.8.777] [Biggar gravestone]

HISLOP, ROBERT, born 1785, a labourer in Port Glasgow, with his wife and family, emigrated via there aboard the Favourite of St John bound for St John, New Brunswick, on 22 October 1815. [PANB.ms.RS23E.19798]

HISLOP, WILLIAM, a saddler in Biggar, 1789. [NRS.CS228.B7.51]

HODGERT, JAMES, formerly a joiner in Glasgow, later in Plattesmouth, Nebraska, in 1874. [NRS.SC20.34.41.42]

HODGSON, JOHN, born 26 January 1781 in Carmunnock, son of Reverend Joseph Hodgson, was educated at Glasgow University, minister at Blantyre from 1809 until his death on 9 February 1832. [F.3.229]

HOGARTH, GEORGE, Lieutenant Colonel of the 26th [Cameronian] Regiment, died in Quebec on 25 July 1854. [EEC.22620]

HOGG, JAMES, a hammerman in Provan, father of James Hogg a smith 'sometime in North America', 1821. [NRS.CS17.1.40/219]

HOGG, JOHN, born 1758 in Dalserf, died at his son's residence on the River Don near Toronto, Canada, on 9 April 1851. [W.XII.1222]

HOGUE, THOMAS, in Bridgeton, applied to settle in Canada on 4 March 1815. [NRS.RH9]

HOOD, ALEXANDER, son of James Hood an Exciseman in Glasgow, brother of Mary Hood in Drygate, Glasgow, died in Montserrat before 1817. [HHG]

HOOD, ANGUS, of the Rutherglen Emigration Society, with his wife, son and two daughters, emigrated via Greenock aboard the Commerce of Greenock, Captain Covendale, bound for Quebec on 11 May 1821. [TNA.CO42.189]

HOOD, HENRY, and son, from Lanark, emigrated via Greenock aboard the Portaferry, bound for Quebec in May 1832. [QM.13.6.1832] [GWS]

HOOD, MATTHEW, a carpenter from Glasgow, settled in the parish of St Paul, Tobago, died in Paris, France, on 10 May 1824, father of Agnes Hood, wife of William Adam a butcher in Kilsyth, Lanarkshire, testament, 1825. [NRS.CC8.8.150]

HOOD, WILLIAM, in 3 Cecil Place, Paisley Road, Glasgow, father of William Hood, born 1858, died at 106 Philip Street. Sydney, New South Wales, Australia, on 16 December 1884. [S.12966]

HOOK, JOHN, born 1745, son of Henry Hook a manufacturer in Glasgow, emigrated to Virginia in 1758, a merchant in Blandford, Va., later in New London, Bedford County, and at Hale's Fort, died 1808. [VMHB.1926]

HOPE, JOHN, son of William Hope in Glasgow, died in Trinidad in 1817. [S.32.17]

HOPE, WILLIAM, a merchant was admitted as a burgess and guildsbrother of Glasgow on 2 February 1797, as married to Jean Lochhead, daughter of John Lochhead a wright, burgess and guilds-brother. [GBR]

HOPKINS, ISABELLA, born 1815, wife of Robert Allan, [1808-1877], a mason, died in Toronto, Canada, on 6 June 1900. [Glassford gravestone]

HORNE, JOHNSTONE, master of the Favourite of Port Glasgow from Greenock to St John, New Brunswick, in 1818 and in 1820. [NRS.E504.15.122]

HORNE, Reverend WILLIAM, late of the United Secession Church in Carnwath, died in Yorktown, Delaware County, Indiana, on 17 December 1848. [EC.28230] [SG.18.1793] [WXVIII.1793]

HOUSTON, ALEXANDER, master of the Phoenix of Glasgow from Greenock to Jamaica in September 1796. [NRS.E504.15.73]

HOUSTON, ALEXANDER, Governor of Grenada, was admitted as an burgess and guilds-brother of Glasgow on 14 July 1802. [GBR]

HOUSTON, ALEXANDER, a weaver, was admitted as a burgess and guilds-brother of Glasgow on 27 August 1808. [GBR]

HOUSTON, ALEXANDER, son of Alexander Houston a manufacturer in Glasgow, died in St Lucia on 11 November 1821. [DPCA] [AJ.3862]

HOUSTON, JOHN, a gabartman in Port Glasgow, testament, 1817, Comm. Glasgow. [NRS]

HOWIE, ANDREW, guilty of theft, was sentenced in Glasgow to seven years transportation to the colonies in 1815. [NRS.GD1.959]

HUIE, PATRICK, son of James Huie a merchant in Port Glasgow, a merchant in St John's, Newfoundland, in 1819. [NRS.SC53.56.2]

HUME, Dr JOSEPH, in Hamilton, father of Dr William Henry Hume, a surgeon to HM Forces, who died in Barbados on 18 November 1827. [S.844.98] [AJ.4178]

HUNTER, ANDREW, born 1777 in Glasgow, a cotton machine maker who died in Savanna, Georgia, on 16 August 1807. [Savanna Death Register]

HUNTER, HUGH, of the Barrowfield Road Emigration Society, with his wife and family, emigrated via Greenock aboard the George Canning, Captain Potter, bound for Quebec on 14 April 1821. [TNA.CO42.189]

HUNTER, JAMES, with three children, from Glasgow, emigrated via Greenock aboard the Portaferry, bound for Quebec in May 1832. [QM.13.6.1832] [GWS]

HUNTER, JOHN M., a merchant from Glasgow, died in Malaga, Spain, on 17 September 1820. [SM.86.479]

HUNTER, RICHARD, a skipper in Port Glasgow, testament, 1803, Comm. Glasgow. [NRS]

HUNTER, ROBERT, a mariner in Port Glasgow, testament, 1819, Comm. Glasgow. [NRS]

HUNTER, ROBERT, a merchant in Philadelphia, Pennsylvania, son and heir of William Hunter a merchant in Glasgow, 1806. [NRS.S/H]

HUNTER, THOMAS, born 1790 in Glasgow, a blacksmith in Charleston, South Carolina, was naturalised on 8 October 1813. [NARA.M1183.1]

HUNTER, THOMAS, a weaver and manufacturer in North Albion Street, Glasgow, was admitted as a burgess and guilds-brother of Glasgow on 18 November 1822, as eldest son of Thomas Hunter a weaver, burgess and guilds-brother. [GBR]

HUNTER, WILLIAM, a mariner in Port Glasgow, testament, 1819, Comm. Glasgow. [NRS]

HUTCHISON, HENRY, a shipowner in Philadelphia, Pennsylvania, uncle and heir of John MacFarlane an innkeeper in Glasgow, 1837. [NRS.S/H]

HUTCHISON, HUGH, late skipper in Port Glasgow, testament, 1816, Comm. Glasgow. [NRS]

HUTCHISON, MARY, from Glasgow, married William Gray from Trinidad, in Portobello, [Midlothian?], in 1810. [EA.4868.125]

HUTCHISON, or AULD, MARY, probably from Lanark, settled in Adelaide, South Australia, by 1855. [NRS.S/H]

HUTCHISON, THOMAS, a shoemaker in Dillarburn, Lesmahagow, was accused of discharging firearms in 1827. [NRS.AD14.27.91]

HYDE, JAMES, a woodcutter in Honduras, probably from Greenock, appointed James MacArthur a merchant in Glasgow, as his attorney on 8 October 1814. [NRS.RD5.59.253]

IMRIE, GEORGE, born 1803, died in Tobago in 1828. [Maryhill grave]

INGLIS, ANTHONY, an accountant from Glasgow, was drowned in the River Suhane, Lunenburg, Nova Scotia, 17 May 1846. [W.VII.705]

INGLIS, JAMES, born 1773, son of Cornelius Inglis, a surgeon, and his wife Euphemia Weir in Lanark, late of Kingston, Jamaica, died in Walthamstow, Essex, England, on 5 November 1814. [Lanark grave]

INGLIS, JAMES, in Glasgow, applied to settle in Canada on 25 February 1815. [NRS.RH9]

INGLIS, JOHN, from Douglas, Lanarkshire, a shopkeeper in New York from 1777, a member of the St Andrew's Society of New York in 1785. [NRS.GD1.46] [ANY]

INGLIS, JOHN, from Carnwath, later in Fayette County, Kentucky, returned to Carnwath by 1816. [NRS.CS17.1.36/132]

INGLIS, ROBERT, a blacksmith from Wishaw, settled in Luzerne County, Pennsylvania, letters, 1850s. [NLS.ms10,331.16-17]

INGLIS, THOMAS, MD, a surgeon in Glasgow, brother and heir of James Inglis in Barrataria, Louisiana, 1836. [NRS.S/H]

INGRAM, JAMES, a merchant from Glasgow, later in Virginia in 1798. [NRS.CS17.1.17/274]

INNES, FRANCES, daughter of Alexander Innes a surgeon in St Kitts, wife of Andrew Buchanan a merchant in Glasgow, ded in January 1785, testament, 1802, Comm. Glasgow. [NRS]

IRVINE, ISABEL, daughter of the deceased John Irvine, principal clerk to the Chancery of Scotland, and spouse of William Kirkpatrick in Huntsfield near Biggar, versus the said William Kirkpatrick, a Process of Adherence, dated 1794. [NRS.CC8.6.932]

IRVIN, RICHARD JOHN, born 1799, son of William Irvin a merchant in Glasgow, a student at Glasgow University in 1810, a merchant in New York, died at Oyster Bay, Long Island, N.Y., on 27 June 1858. [MAGU][ANY]

IRVIN, WILLIAM, a merchant, was admitted as a burgess and guilds-brother of Glasgow on 31 March 1808, by right of his wife Agnes Young, daughter of David Young a merchant, burgess and guilds-brother. [GBR]

ISAAC, ROBERT, born 1780 in Glasgow, died in Georgia on 16 October 1827. [Georgia gravestone][Georgia Republican, 16.10.1827]

ISAAC, WILLIAM, a merchant, was admitted as a burgess and guilds-brother of Glasgow on 30 January 1829 as eldest son of William Isaac a cordiner, burgess and guilds-brother. [GBR]

IVISON, HENRY, born 1808 in Glasgow, emigrated to America in 1820, a publisher in New York, died there in 1884. [TSA]

JACK, Dr DAVID, son of Dr Jack in Hamilton, died in Portsmouth, Virginia, on 3 May 1792. [EEC.11561]

JACK, THOMAS, a merchant in Virginia, died in Airdrie House, New Monklands, testament, 22 September 1814, Comm. Hamilton. [NRS]

JACK, WILLIAM, born 1782, a labourer in Bellshill, emigrated on board the George of New York bound for New York on 12 August 1807. [TNA.PC1.3790]

JACKSON, SUSANNA, in Jamaica, grand-daughter and heir of Alexander Campbell a merchant in Glasgow, 1817. [NRS.S/H]

JAFFREY, JOHN, a mercantile agent in Antigua Place, Glasgow, was admitted as a burgess and guilds-brother of Glasgow, by right of his wife Ellison Lockhart, daughter of Robert Lockhart a merchant, burgess and guilds-brother. [GBR]

JAFFRAY, ROBERT, from Glasgow, emigrated via Greenock aboard the Portaferry, bound for Quebec in May 1832. [QM.13.6.1832] [GWS]

JAMIESON, HUGH, in Anderston, a bond, 1 February 1841. [NRS.RD29.3.23]

JAMIESON, JAMES, a merchant in Demerara, appointed Alexander McDonald, a merchant in Glasgow, as his attorney and factor, on 22 April 1811. [NRS.RD5.88.666]

JAMIESON, JOHN, born 22 June 1794 in Abington, son of James Jamieson and his wife Mary Gillespie, a partner in Gillespie, Moffat and Company in Montreal, died in Edinburgh on 1 January 1848. [Biggar gravestone]

JAMIESON, JOHN, born 1798 in Glasgow, settled in Pictou, Nova Scotia, in 1826, died in Montreal, Quebec, on 11 August 1834. [AR.20.9.1834]

JAMIESON, JOHN, born 1831, son of John Jamieson in Glasgow, died on 26 November 1850, was buried in the British Cemetery, Funchal, Madeira. [ARM]

JAMIESON, ROBERT, born 20 January 1851 in Glasgow, son of Reverend Robert Jamieson and his wife Eliza, died in Canada on 7 May 1891. [F.3.464]

JARVIE, WALTER, with his wife and child, from Kirkintilloch, emigrated via Greenock aboard the Portaferry, bound for Quebec in May 1832. [QM.13.6.1832] [GWS]

JASON, PETER, master of the Susannah of Port Glasgow from Port Glasgow to Chaleur Bay, New Brunswick, in 1820. [NRS.E504.28.108]

JOHNSTON, ADAM, an overseer in the parish of St Elizabeth, Jamaica, brother of John Johnston a coachbuilder in Glasgow, died in July 1795, testament, 1796. [NRS.CC8.8.130]

JOHNSTON, AGNES, in Glasgow, daughter and heir of Euphemia Cheyne, wife of James Johnston in Boston, USA, 1846. [NRS.S/H]

JOHNSTONE, Mrs ALICE, born 1786, wife of Reverend John Johnston late of Glasgow, died in Jersey City, New Jersey, on 26 July 1849. [SG.18.1847]

JOHNSTON, ANDREW, a merchant in New York, brother and heir of his sister Agnes Johnston or Dempster, daughter of Michael Johnston a merchant in Glasgow, 1856. [NRS.S/H]

JOHNSTON, ARCHIBALD, from Glasgow, died in Charleston, South Carolina, on 28 December 1807. [SM.70.317]

JOHNSTON, ARCHIBALD SIMPSON, born 1784 in Port Glasgow, son of Adam Johnson, was educated at Glasgow University in 1799, a planter in South Carolina, was naturalised on 23 August 1813, died in Roshi, S.C., on 15 August 1819. [NARA.M1183.1] [MAGU]

JOHNSTON, ARCHIBALD, a builder in Glasgow, also contractor for the public buildings in Ayr was admitted as a burgess and freeman of Ayr on 9 April 1828. [ABR]

JOHNSTON, CLEMENT, in Glasgow, applied to settle in Canada on 28 February 1815. [NRS.RH9]

JOHNSTON, DAVID, a manufacturer in Glasgow, emigrated to America in 1816. [NRS.CS36.17.88]

JOHNSTON, GEORGE, master of the Oscar of Glasgow from Greenock to Newfoundland in 1815. [NRS.E504.15.109]

JOHNSTON, JAMES, of the Brownfield and Anderston Emigration Society, emigrated via Greenock on board the Earl of Buckinghamshire, Captain Johnston, bound for Quebec on 29 April 1821, with his wife, son and daughter, was granted land in Ramsay, Upper Canada, on 26 July 1821. [TNA.CO42.189] [PAO]

JOHNSTON, JAMES, in Montreal, Quebec, son and heir of James Johnston, a spirit merchant in Glasgow, who died 3 April 1854. [NRS.S/H]

JOHNSTON, JOHN, a farmer in Cambusnethan, Lanarkshire, died 9 April 1863, father of John Yuill Johnston in Pietermaritzburg, Natal, South Africa. [NRS.S/H.1881]

JOHNSTON, WILLIAM, an ironmonger and merchant, was admitted as a burgess and guilds-brother of Glasgow, on 24 August 1795 having served his apprenticeship with James Sword a merchant, burgess and guilds-brother. [NRS.S/H]

JOHNSTON, WILLIAM, a merchant from Glasgow, in New York around 1804. [NRS.CS17.1.23/472]

JOHNSTONE, WILLIAM, third son of James Johnstone a tanner in Glasgow, died in New York in 1817. [S.1.34]

JOHNSTON, Captain, master of the Clansman of Glasgow bund from Glasgow with passengers to Quebec in 1849. [QM.23.6.1849]

JOPE, ROBERT, born 1823, from Glasgow, emigrated to America in 1855, declared his intention to naturalise on 20 October 1856. [Norfolk County Circuit Records, Virginia]

JOPP, KEITH, a merchant in Jamaica, co-owner of the Magnet of Glasgow in 1800. [NRS.CE60.11.6/18]

KALLEY, ROBERT, a merchant in Glasgow, married Mary Boyd from Jamaica on 3 August 1795. [GM.65.702]

KAY, DAVID, in Kinsman township, Ohio, son and heir of Margaret Murray, wife of David Kay a merchant in Leith later in Glasgow, who died 7 February 1854. [NRS.S/H]

KELLOCK, JAMES, in New York, son and heir of John Kellock a mason in Coatbridge, who died 1 January 1863. [NRS.S/H]

KELLY, GEORGE, master of the Sir Edward Pellew of Glasgow, from Greenock to Quebec in 1814, and from Greenock to New Brunswick in 1814. [NRS.E504.15.99/103/106]

KENNEDY, ANGUS, son of Daniel Kennedy in Glasgow, died in St Lucie, Jamaica, in 1802. [EA.4042.02][GkAd.75]

KENNEDY, ARCHIBALD, son of Daniel Kennedy in Glasgow, died in Norfolk, Virginia, in 1802. [EA.4042.02] [GkAd.75]

KENNEDY, Dr D., born in Glasgow, died in Waterloo, Jamaica, on 25 November 1827. [BM.23.664] [AJ.4178]

KENNEDY, HUGH, baptised on 1 November 1768 in Glasgow, son of Daniel Kennedy and his wife Mary Brodie, died in Philadelphia, Pennsylvania, in 1803. [GM.73.86] [EA.4042.02][GkAd.75]

KENNEDY, HUGH, a gardener, was admitted as a burgess and guilds-brother of Glasgow on 23 August 1805, having served an apprenticeship under Daniel Kennedy a gardener, burgess and guilds-brother. [GBR]

KENT, JOHN, of the Glasgow Trongate Emigration Society, with his wife and family, emigrated via Greenock aboard the David of London, master David Gemmil, bound for Quebec on 19 May 1821. [TNA.CO42.189]

KERR, JOHN, son of Reverend Kerr in Carmunnock, died in Jamaica in 1811. [EA]

KERR, JOHN, born 1800 in Glasgow, emigrated via Greenock to America, was naturalised in New York on 27 January 1827. [NY Court of Common Pleas]

KERR, JOHN, a merchant in Toronto, Canada, later in California, son and heir of James Kerr, an engraver in Glasgow, who died 26 October 1841; also, heir to his sister Isabella Margaret Kerr in Glasgow, who died 8 December 1862. [NRS.S/H]

KERR, JOHN, of Dalmuir House, Glasgow, born 1788, died in Rome on 3 April 1848. [Protestant Cemetery gravestone, Rome]

KEVAN, WILLIAM, born 1812, a merchant in Glasgow, died in Madeira on 17 December 1840. [W.II.106]

KIDD, JAMES, agent for the National Bank of Scotland in Airdrie, 1849. [POD]

KIDSTON, WILLIAM, a merchant in 19 Queen Street, Glasgow, was admitted as a burgess and guilds-brother of Glasgow on 28 September 1833 as eldest son of Richard Kidston a merchant, burgess and guilds-brother. [GBR]

KIDSTON, Captain, master of the Hope of Glasgow from Glasgow with passengers in 1851. [GCA.TCN.26/5]

KIGGINS, JAMES, from Pollockshaws, Glasgow, emigrated to USA in July 1845, settled in Pennsylvania. [Boston Pilot, 8.11.1845]

KILPATRICK, EPHRAIM, of the Bridgeton Canadian Emigration Society, with his wife and family, emigrated via Greenock aboard the George Canning, Captain Potter, bound for Quebec on 14 April 1821. [TNA.CO42.189]

KILPATRICK, JOHN, President of the Bridgeton Canadian Emigration Society, with his wife and family, emigrated via Greenock aboard the George Canning, Captain Potter, bound for Quebec on 14 April 1821. [TNA.CO42.189]

KING, HENRY CURZON, born 1811, second son of John King of Springbank, Port Glasgow, died in Kingston, Jamaica, on 14 November 1830. [GrA.11.2.1831]

KING, JAMES, of the Rutherglen Emigration Society, emigrated via Greenock aboard the Commerce of Greenock, Captain Covendale, bound for Quebec on 11 May 1821, was granted land in Lanark, Upper Canada, on 22 August 1821. [TNA.CO42.189] [PAO]

KING, JAMES, agent for the Union Bank of Scotland in Port Glasgow in 1849. [POD]

KING, JOHN, in St Pierre, Martinique, son of John King a cooper in Port Glasgow, died abroad on 25 December 1799, testament, 1807. [NRS.CC8.8.137]

KING, ROBERT, MD, from Glasgow, died in Paris, France, on 22 March 1829. [S.968]

KINLAY, WILLIAM, born 1807 in Kirkintilloch, died and was buries in the British Cemetery, Funchal, Madeira, on 6 October 1844. [ARM]

KINNEAR, JOHN, master of the Hopewell of Glasgow, testament, 1814, Comm. Glasgow. [NRS]

KIPPEN, WILLIAM, a merchant in Glasgow, was admitted as a burgess and freeman of Ayr on 9 August 1815. [ABR]

KIRKWOOD, JAMES, a grocer from Glasgow, and his wife Cecilia Colquhoun, settled in America by 1806. [NRS.CS17.1.25/475]

KIRKWOOD, ROBERT, born 1804, from Kirkintilloch, died in Montreal, Quebec, on 15 May 1840. [GSP.684]

KNOX, ROBERT DADE, in Wilkes County, Georgia, son of Robert Knox a merchant in Virginia, grandson of John Knox a shipwright in Port Glasgow in 1821. [NRS.CS17.1.40/183]; a deed, 1829. [NRS.RD5.398.456]

KNOX, WALTER, born 1770 in Glasgow, a house carpenter who was naturalised in South Carolina on 14 October 1806. [NARA.M1183.1]

KYLE, WILLIAM, of the Glasgow Trongate Emigration Society, with his wife and family, emigrated via Greenock aboard the David of London, master David Gemmil, bound for Quebec on 19 May 1821. [TNA.CO42.189]

LADE, DAVID, a merchant of Wotherspoon and Lade, spirit dealers in Stirling Street, Glasgow, was admitted as a burgess and guilds-brother of Glasgow on 19 August 1828, by right of his wife Catherine Carswell, daughter of William Carswell a wright, burgess and guilds-brother. [GBR]

LAING, JOHN, died 30 August 1808 in Dominica, father of Susan Laing in Stonehouse. [NRS.S/H]

LAIRD, JAMES, born 1789, a labourer in Port Glasgow, emigrated from there aboard the Favourite of St John bound for St John, New Brunswick on 22 October 1815. [PANB.ms.RS23e.19798]

LAIRD, JOHN, a merchant in Georgetown, Maryland, son of William Laird a merchant in Port Glasgow, appointed George Oswald of Scotstoun, Glasgow, Alexander Oswald of Shieldhall, and Harry Robertson a merchant in Glasgow as his factors and attornies, on 8 November 1794. [NRS.RD3.269.640]; 1796, 1813, [NRS.CS17.1.15/419; NRAS.0623.TMJ.353; SC58.59.3.211]

LAIRD, WILLIAM, son of David Laird in Glasgow, died in Mobile, Alabama, on 13 May 1849. [SG.18.1827]

LAIRDAL, WILLIAM, a handloom weaver in 57 Nelson Street, Glasgow, applied to settle in Canada on 14 April 1827. [TNA.CO384.5.919]

LAMB, ROBERT, a manufacturer from Glasgow, settled in America by 1808. [NRS.CS17.1.27/344]

LAMB, ROBERT, from Hamilton, settled in Fredericton, New Brunswick, by 1815. [NRS.SC37.59.3/102]

LAMOND, JEAN, spouse of William Walker jr, a manufacturer in Glasgow, died on 14 September 1822 [SM.90.632]

LAMONT, JOHN, a shipmaster in Port Glasgow, testament, 1790, Comm. Glasgow. [NRS]

LANG, GILBERT, in Chapel Printfield, Glasgow, applied to settle in Canada, on 25 February 1827. [TNA.CO384.5.907]

LANG, JOHN, born 9 January 1808 in Glasgow, son of Gilbert Lang and his wife Elizabeth McFie, a Colonel of the 36th Bengal Native Infantry, died in London, England, on 10 March 1882. [BA.3.14]

LANG, MARY, died 27 May 1832, wife of William Rennie in Kilsyth. [NRS.S/H.1867]

LANG, WALTER, a merchant, was admitted as a burgess and guilds-brother of Glasgow on 16 September 1802, as eldest son of Walter Lang a baker, burgess and guilds-brother. [GBR]

LANG, WALTER, a merchant, son of Walter Lang a magistrate in Glasgow, died in Sydney, Australia, on 30 March 1816. [S.1.23]

LANG, WILLIAM, a merchant, was admitted as a burgess and guilds-brother of Glasgow on 30 January 1790, as younger son of William Lang a merchant, burgess and guilds-brother. [GBR]

LANG, WILLIAM, born 1771 in Glasgow, settled in Portsmouth, New Hampshire, married Maria Bailey in New York on 3 January 1796, a merchant in N.Y. until 1844, died in Wyoming, Massachusetts, on 27 August 1849. [ANY]

LANG, WILLIAM, from Glasgow, died in Milwaukee, Wisconsin, on 16 January 1850. [W.1086]

LANGWELL, Captain, master of the Tay of Glasgow with passengers, bound from Greenock to Quebec in June 1843. [LCL]

LAPSLEY, SARAH OGDEN, daughter of William Lapsley in Montreal, Quebec, grand-daughter and heir of William Lapsley a grocer in Glasgow, 1819. [NRS.S/H]

LARNE, Captain, master of the Levant of Glasgow, from the Clyde on 12 January 1846 bound for Sydney, New South Wales, landed there on 22 May 1846. [LCL.4200]

LAURIE, CATHERINE, born 1786, in Rutherglen, wife of Robert Malcolm, a weaver in Waterbrae, Bridge Street, Paisley, was accused of bigamy with Robert Leslie in Rutherglen in 1836. [NRS.AD14.36.274]

LAURIE, JOHN, of the Hamilton Emigration Society, with his wife, four sons, and four daughters, emigrated via Greenock on board the Commerce of Greenock, Captain Coverdale, bound for Quebec on 11 May 1821, was granted land in Dalhousie, Upper Canada, on 15 July 1821. [TNA.CO42.89] [PAO]

LAW, ALEXANDER, born 1782, son of James Law in Glasgow, died in Trinidad in 1802. [AJ.2854]

LAW, WILLIAM, of the Strathaven and Kilbride Emigration Society, emigrated via Greenock aboard the George Canning, Captain Potter, bound for Quebec on 14 April 1821. [TNA.CO42.189]

LAWRIE, Captain, of the Rebecca of Glasgow from Greenock with passengers bound for Quebec, 1831-1832, shipwrecked in the St Lawrence River in 1832. [QM]

LAWSON, ALEXANDER, born at Ravenstruther, Carstairs, on 19 November 1773, emigrated to America in 1794, an engraver in Philadelphia, Pennsylvania, died there on 22 August 1846. [WA]

LAWSON, GEORGE, from Glasgow, died at Aux Cayes, St Domingo, on 10 June 1820. [AJ.3792]

LAWSON, JAMES, a merchant, was admitted as a burgess and guildsbrother of Glasgow on 27 August 1808. [GBR]

LAWSON, JAMES, born 9 November 1799, son of James Lawson a merchant in Glasgow, a student at Glasgow University in 1812, a merchant in USA from 1815 until 1826, later a journalist and insurance broker in New York, died in Yonkers, N.Y., on 20 March 1880. [MAGU][ANY]; son and heir of John Lawson, a merchant in Glasgow, 1851. [NRS.S/H]

LAWSON, JOHN, in Canada, son and heir of Mary Wright, wife of William Wright in Glasgow, 1825. [NRS.S/H]

LAWSON, MATTHEW, a butcher in Glasgow, testament, 1820. Comm. Glasgow. [NRS]

LAWSON, OSCAR, born 1808 in Lanark, later a merchant in New York, died in Brooklyn, N.Y., on 15 October 1852. [ANY]

LAWSON, ROBERT, born 1827, Rector of Melbourne Academy, New South Wales, Australia, died at sea on 3 April 1869. [Walston grave]

LAWSON, WILLIAM, in Indiana, son and heir of George Lawson of Cuparhead in Lanarkshire, who died in November 1829. [NRS.S/H]

LAWSON, Captain, master of the Stephane of Glasgow from Glasgow to Melbourne, Victoria, Australia, landed there on 16 May 1854. [LCL.4288/4322]

LEADBETTER, ALEXANDER, from Glasgow, a divinity student in 1824, emigrated to America. [AUPC]

LEARMONTH, ALEXANDER, a weaver in Gateside, Hamilton, a former soldier of the 15th Regiment of Foot, applied to settle in Canada on 23 March 1827. [TNA.CO.384.5.915]

LECKIE, DAVID, of the Glasgow Trongate Emigration Society, with his wife and family, emigrated via Greenock aboard the David of London, master David Gemmil, bound for Quebec on 19 May 1821. [TNA.CO42.189]

LECKIE, EMMELINE, wife of John Goodrick Hatton in Portsmouth, Virginia, was heir to Ralph Foster in Drummoyne who died in February 1810. [NRS.S/H]

LEES, ALEXANDER, jr., a weaver from Glasgow, settled in New York, grandson and heir of Charles Patterson a portioner in Glasgow, who died 6 October 1823. [NRS.S/H]

LEIPER, THOMAS, born 1745 in Strathaven, a merchant in Philadelphia, Pennsylvania, died in 1825. [S]; third son of Thomas Leiper and his wife Helen Hamilton, a merchant, emigrated to Maryland in 1763, settled in Philadelphia, Pennsylvania, in 1765, a tobacco merchant, died in Delaware County or in Philadelphia on 6 July 1825. [AP][WA]

LEISHMAN, ROBERT, born 1791, a labourer in Port Glasgow, emigrated via there aboard the Favourite of St John bound for St John, New Brunswick, on 22 October 1815. [PANB.ms.RS23E.19798]

LEITCH, JAMES, a weaver from Glasgow, of the Strathaven and Kilbride Emigration Society, with his wife and family, emigrated via Greenock aboard the George Canning, Captain Potter, bound for Quebec on 14 April 1821. [TNA.CO42.189]; settled in North Sherbrook township, Upper Canada, in 1821. [BPP.2.167]

LEITCH, WILLIAM, Provost of Rutherglen, was accused of celebrating clandestine marriages in 1823. [NRS.AD.14.23.59]

LENNIE, DUNCAN, born 1814 in Glasgow, son of Robert Lennie a merchant, was educated at Glasgow University, a minister in Tobago from 1837 to 1844, died in Northumberland, England, on 12 December 1858. [F.7.671]

LENNOX, MARGARET, was born in 1822 in Chapelton, Avondale, Lanarkshire, wife of Andrew Hamilton in Strathavon, was accused of the murder of Jean Hamilton in Kirk Street Strathavon in 1847. [NRS.AD14.50.49]

LERRIE, HUGH, in North America, son and heir of James Lerrie in Anderston, Glasgow, who died on 17 January 1848. [NRS.S/H]

LESLIE, ROBERT, born 1794 in Glasgow, emigrated via London to America in 1817, married Nancy Gillian Duncan, daughter of Charles Duncan, a merchant in Roslin, Virginia, later a tobacco merchant in Petersburg, Virginia. [DUpp]

LESLIE, THOMAS, of the Bridgeton Canadian Emigration Society, emigrated via Greenock aboard the George Canning, Captain Potter, bound for Quebec on 14 April 1821. [TNA.CO42.189]

LEWARS, JAMES, in Hanover, Ohio, son and heir of Helen Lithgow, wife of John Lewars a weaver in Lanark, 1853. [NRS.S/H]

LEWIS, JAMES, son of James Lewis a gentleman in Spanish Town, Jamaica, matriculated at Glasgow University in 1793. [MAGU]

LEWIS, JAMES, DD, born 1805 in Glasgow, a minister of the Free Church of Scotland in Leith and in Rome, died in Rome in 1872. [Protestant Cemetery gravestone, Rome]

LIDDLE, ANDREW, of the Camlachie Emigration Society, with his wife, two sons, and two daughters, emigrated via Greenock on board the Commerce of Greenock, Captain Coverdale, bound for Quebec on 11 May 1821, was granted land in Lanark, Upper Canada, on 1 August 1821. [TNA.CO42.89] [PAO]

LILLIE, GEORGE, a merchant of George Lillie and Company, Brazilian merchants, was admitted as a burgess and guilds-brother of Glasgow 78 on 10 July 1828, as younger son of David Lillie, a merchant burgess and guilds-brother. [GBR]

LINDSAY, JAMES, from Glasgow, married Agnes Patterson from Cockburnspath, Berwickshire, in New York, in 1860. [DC.23491]

LINDSAY, JOHN, an auctioneer in Glasgow, was admitted as a burgess and guilds-brother of Ayr on 18 March 1807. [ABR]

LINDSAY, JOHN, a merchant in Grenada, and John Todd a merchant on Carriacou, appointed Adam Crooks in Glasgow as their attorney on 17 December 1812. [NRS.RD5.25.292]

LINDSAY, JOHN, born 1821, son of David Lindsay and his wife Helen Hastie, died in Glenelg, South Australia, in May 1898. [Lanark gravestone]

LINDSAY, ROBERT, born 1759, died in Lanarkshire on 1 June 1836, father of John Lindsay in Pictou, Nova Scotia. [Acadian Recorder, 24.9.1836]

LINDSAY, WILLIAM, of the Wishaw Emigration Society with his wife and family, emigrated via Greenock aboard the David of London, master David Gemmill, bound for Quebec on 19 May 1821. [TNA.CO42.189]

KING, JAMES, jr., a shipmaster and merchant in Port Glasgow, testament, 1798, Comm. Glasgow. [NRS]

LISTON, ROBERT, of Damhead, married Henrietta Merchant, daughter of Nathaniel Merchant in Antigua, in St Andrew's Episcopal Church in Glasgow on 27 February 1796. [Scottish Antiquary.X.23]

LITHGOW, ALEXANDER, in Virginia, brother and heir of Mary Lithgow wife of James Wilson, an innkeeper in Douglas, 1793. [NRS.S/H]

LITT, THOMAS, a merchant from Glasgow, died in Madeira on 23 February 1821, testament, 1823, Comm. Dumfries. [NRS]

LITTLE, BRYCE, minister in Covington, dead by 1822, uncle of William Little in Tennessee, his heir. [NRS.S/H]

LIVINGSTONE, Mrs JEAN, wife of John Livngstone a collier in Bellahouston, niece and heir of Thomas Gordon a wright in Jamaica, 1799. [NRS.S/H]

LIVINGSTONE, JOHN, born in November 1771, a spinner from near Glasgow, with his wife and children, landed in America on 1 May 1811, settled in Whitestown, Oneida County, New York. [1812]

LOCKHART, JOHN, of the Lesmahagow Emigration Society, with his wife and three daughters, emigrated to Canada on the Earl of Buckinghamshire, Captain Johnston, on 29 April 1821, was granted land in Ramsay, Upper Canada, on 31 July 1821. [TNA.CO42.189] [PAO]

LOCKHART, RICHARD DICKSON, born 31 March 1807 in Glasgow, son of Reverend John Lockhart and his wife Elizabeth Gibson, an Ensign of the 68th Bengal Native Infantry, was drowned at Sandoway, Arakan, Burma, on 27 December 1826. [BA.3.72]

LOCKHART, WILLIAM, born 28 September 1787 in Cambusnethan, Lanarkshire, son of Reverend John Lockhart and his wife Elizabeth Dinwiddie, a Brevet Captain of the 17th Bengal Native Infantry, died in Milton Lockhart on 25 November 1856. [BA.3.72]

LOCHHEAD, ROBERT, born 1835 in Shotts, married Jean Carswell, born 1835 in North Linridge, married in 1854. [Shotts OPR]

LOCHHEAD, WILLIAM, of the Glasgow Wrights Emigration Society, with his wife and family, emigrated via Greenock aboard the George Canning, Captain Potter, bound for Quebec on 14 April 1821. [TNA.CO42.189]

LOCHEAD, WILLIAM, son of William Lochead a craftsman in Bridgeton, Glasgow, a student at Glasgow University in 1816, later a theological student from 1821 to 1824, settled in Kingston, Canada, later in Albany, New York. [MAGU]

LOCKHART, NORMAN, of Tarbrax, died 5 March 1853, father of Alexander MacDonald Lockhart in Canada West. [NRS.S/H]

LOCKHART, WILLIAM, born 28 September 1787 in Cambusnethan, son of Reverend John Lockhart and his wife Elizabeth Dinwiddie, a Brevet Captain of the 17th Bengal Native Infantry, died on 25 November 1856 in Milton Lockhart. [BA.3.72]

LOGAN, JEAN, in Glasgow, widow of Alexander Buchanan of Newport, Jamaica, a testament, 1823, Comm. Glasgow. [NRS]

LOGAN, JOHN, of Eastshield, Carnwath, father of John W. Logan who died on the voyage home from Buenos Ayres, Argentina, on 9 August 1867. [S.7518]

LOGAN, WALTER, Customs Controller in Perth Amboy, New Jersey, was admitted as a burgess and guilds-brother of Glasgow, as son of Reverend John Logan minister of East Kilpatrick husband of Margaret Murdoch, daughter of Peter Murdoch, a merchant, burgess and guilds-brother of Glasgow, 10 June 1784. [GBR]

LOGAN, WILLIAM, born 1792, died 8 March 1862, husband of Jane Johnstone, born 1792, died 9 March 1864, 'founders of the Logan and Johnston Orphan School'. [Ramshorn gravestone]

LOGAN, WILLIAM, in Lanark, died 1 September 1858, father of John Logan a saddler in America, NRS.S/H]

LOGAN, Captain, master of the Serostris of Glasgow bound from Glasgow with passengers for Quebec in 1851. [BPP]

LOTTIMER, WILLIAM, born 1815 in Glasgow, settled in New York during 1844, a merchant who died in Fishkill, N.Y., on 7 October 1876. [ANY]

LOVE, ROBERT, of the Camlachie Emigration Society, with his wife, two sons, and a daughter, emigrated via Greenock on board the Commerce of Greenock, Captain Coverdale, bound for Quebec on 11 May 1821, was granted land in Sherbrook, Upper Canada, on 1 August 1821. [TNA.CO42.89] [PAO]

LOW, JANET, daughter of the deceased Thomas Low, a feuar in Biggar, and spouse of James Rennie, a tailor in Glasgow, who married in 1785, versus said James Rennie in 1795. [NRS.CS]

LUSK, ARCHIBALD, a seaman aboard the schooner Albion of Glasgow testament, 1823, Comm. Glasgow. [NRS]

LUSK, JAMES, a shipmaster in Port Glasgow, testament, 1797, Comm. Glasgow. [NRS]

LYON, R., master of the Alexander of Glasgow from Greenock bound for Prince Edward Island, Canada, in 1820. [NRS.E504.15.129]

MCADAM, JAMES, a merchant in Charleston, South Carolina, later in Glasgow by 1829. [NRS.RD5.379.655]

MCADAM, JOHN, son of Peter McAdam a merchant in Glasgow, was educated at Glasgow University in 1810, died on Sullivan's Island, Charleston, South Carolina, on 15 July 1823. [MAGU]

MCALLISTER, WILLIAM, from Glasgow, settled in America by 1803. [NRS.AC7.76]

MCALPIN, ANDREW, of the Brownfield and Anderston Emigration Society, emigrated via Greenock on board the Earl of Buckinghamshire, Captain Johnston, bound for Quebec on 29 April 1821, with his wife, two sons and two daughters, was granted land in Sherbrook, Upper Canada, on 31 July 1821. [TNA.CO42.189] [PAO]

MCALPIN, ARCHIBALD, born 1772 in Glasgow, settled in South Carolina and later in Georgia, died in Savanna, Georgia, in 1822. [GFC.28.9.1822]

MCALPIN, JAMES, of the Glasgow Trongate Emigration Society, emigrated via Greenock aboard the David of London, master David Gemmil, bound for Quebec on 19 May 1821. [TNA.CO42.189]

MCALPINE, ROBERT, MD, from Lanarkshire, took the Oath of Allegiance in Princess Anne County, Virginia, on 2 June 1823. [NARA]

MCARTHUR, JAMES, born 1824 in Glasgow, died in New Orleans, Louisiana, on 14 September 1853. [QCG]

MCARTHUR, JOHN, in Glasgow, applied to settle in Canada on 27 February 1815. [NRS.RH9]

MCARTHUR, J., master of the Ottawa of Glasgow bound from Glasgow with passengers for Quebec in 1851. [SRA.T/CN.26/5]

MCAUSLAN, JOHN, from Glasgow, emigrated via Liverpool to Montreal, Quebec, in June 1833. [SG.2.152]

MCAUSLAND, ROBERT, a merchant in Glasgow, later in Newfoundland, 1783. [NRS.CS17.1.172/212; CS17.1.9/230]

MCBEAN, AENEAS, the younger of Tomatin, a merchant in Glasgow, died in St Thomas, Danish West Indies, in 1810. [EA.4873.167]

MCBEATH, ANDREW, of the St John's Parish Emigration Society, with his wife, son and two daughters, emigrated via Greenock aboard the Commerce of Greenock, Captain Covendale, bound for Quebec on 11 May 1821, was granted land in Lanark, Upper Canada, on 11 August 1821. [TNA.CO42.189] [PAO]

MCBRAYNE, JOHN BURNS, a merchant of McBrayne and McIndoe merchants and ship agents of 57 Buchanan Street, Glasgow, was admitted as a burgess and guilds-brother of Glasgow on 9 August 1842, as younger son of David McBrayne, a merchant, burgess and guilds-brother of Glasgow. [GBR]

MCCAA, WILLIAM, in Newton Douglas, was appointed attorney by Hector McKenzie, in Bath, Steuben County, New York, later in Philadelphia, Pennsylvania, on 15 July 1796. [NRS.RD4.263.834]

MCCALL, ARCHIBALD, born 28 April 1734, son of Samuel McCall, a merchant in Glasgow, and his wife Margaret Adams, settled in Essex County, Virginia, as a merchant by 1759, husband of Catherine Flood, died in October 1814. [SOF]

MCCALL, JOHN, only son of John McCall formerly a merchant in Jamaica, matriculated at Glasgow University in 1813. [MAGU]

MCCALL, JOHN, born 1 April 1771, second son of John McCall, a merchant in Glasgow, and his wife Helen Cross, died in Castries, St Lucia, on 3 February 1821. [SOF]

MCCALL, JOHN, a skipper in Glasgow, testament, 1806, Comm. Glasgow. [NRS]

MCCALL, JOHN, from Glasgow, emigrated via Liverpool aboard the Roscoe bound for New York in 1833, a merchant in New York from 1833 to 1851, returned to Glasgow. [ANY]

MCCALL, WILLIAM, born 1777, fourth son of George McCall, a merchant in Glasgow, and his wife Mary Smellie, died in Jamaica on 14 August 1802. [JRG]

MCCALLUM, JAMES, of the Abercrombie Emigration Society, with his wife and family, emigrated via Greenock aboard the David of London, master David Gemmil, bound for Quebec on 19 May 1821. [TNA.CO42.189]

MCCALLUM, JOHN, in Glasgow, applied to settle in Canada on 4 March 1815. [NRS.RH9]

MCCALLUM, WILLIAM, of the Camlachie Emigration Society, with his wife, three sons and two daughters, emigrated via Greenock on board the Commerce of Greenock, Captain Coverdale, bound for Quebec on 11 May 1821, was granted land in Lanark, Upper Canada, on 1 August 1821. [TNA.CO42.89] [PAO]

MCCALLUM, WILLIAM, a weaver in 35 Clyde Street, Glasgow, applied to settle in Canada on 1 May 1827. [TNA.CO384.5.987]

MCCALLUM, Captain, master of the Three Bells of Glasgow from Glasgow with passengers bound for Quebec in 1854. [QM.23.5.1854],

MCCAUL, GILBERT, born 1764, a cordiner in Glasgow died 23 May 1842, husband of Janet McFarlan, born 1769, died 11 November 1845. [Ramshorn gravestone]

MCCAUL, JOHN, a merchant in Kingston, Jamaica, co-owner of the Mercury of Glasgow in 1795. [NRS.CE60.11.4/21]

MCCAUL, JOHN, son of John McCaul a merchant in Glasgow, was educated at Glasgow University around 1799, and at Oxford University in 1810, a merchant in St Croix, Danish West Indies, died in Cane Valley there on 16 March 1860. [Car.4.79]

MCCLIMMENT, WILLIAM, master of the Margaret of Glasgow from Greenock to Quebec in 1813. [NRS.E504.15.101]

MCCOIG, DUGALD, born 1803, died in March 1869, husband of Agnes McLean, born 1808, died 11 December 1881, parents of John McCoig, born 1844, died at Cosford, New South Wales, Australia, on 14 August 1893. [Maryhill gravestone]

MACCOLL, DONALD, born 1763 in Appin, Episcopalian Priest at Glasgow Gaelic Church from 1829 until his death on 4 June 1833. [SEC.343]

MCCONNELL, JAMES, of the Camlachie Emigration Society, with his wife, son, and daughter, emigrated via Greenock on board the Commerce of Greenock, Captain Coverdale, bound for Quebec on 11 May 1821, was granted land in Sherbrook, Upper Canada, on 1 August 1821. [TNA.CO42.89] [PAO]

MCCONNELL, RICHARD, of the Camlachie Emigration Society, with his wife, emigrated via Greenock on board the Commerce of Greenock, Captain Coverdale, bound for Quebec on 11 May 1821, was granted land in Sherbrook, Upper Canada, on 1 August 1821. [TNA.CO42.89] [PAO]

MCCOULL, JOHN, heir to Christianna McCoull, daughter of James McCoull a merchant in Glasgow, 1810. [NRS.S/H]

MCCORMICK, DANIEL, a mariner in Port Glasgow, testament, 1795, Comm. Glasgow. [NRS]

MCCRORIE, WILLIAM, a tailor in Warrenton, North Carolina, heir and brother of Grizel McCrorie in Argyle Street, Glasgow, 1827. [NRS.S/H]

MCCULLOCH, JANE, daughter of Andrew McCulloch in Lanarkshire, married Reverend William McCulloch from Truro, Nova Scotia, in Halifax, New Brunswick, on 20 October 1842. [Acadian Recorder, 22.10.1842]

MCCULLOCH, JOHN, of the Spring Bank Emigration Society, emigrated via Greenock aboard the David of London, master David Gemmill, bound for Quebec on 19 May 1821. [TNA.CO42.189]

MCCULLOCH, PETER, of the Spring Bank Emigration Society with his wife and family, emigrated via Greenock aboard the David of London, master David Gemmill, bound for Quebec on 19 May 1821. [TNA.CO42.189]

MCCULLOCH, THOMAS, a Loyalist in Norfolk, Virginia, 1783, [TNA.AO.12.109.200]; later in Westfield, Bothwell, testament, 6 January 1795, Comm. Glasgow. [NRS]

MCDONALD, ALEXANDER, late of Kingston, Jamaica, died 16 June 1840, husband of Jane Houston, who died in Glasgow on 16 February 1836. [Greenock West gravestone]

MCDONALD, ANNE, eldest daughter of Robert McDonald in Glasgow, married Reverend Thomas Clark Wilson of New Perth, Canada, in Quebec on 1 October 1832. [EEC.18875]

MCDONALD, CHARLES, master of the Sir Edward Pellew of Glasgow, from Greenock to Newfoundland in 1813. [NRS.E504.15.99]

MACDONALD, Sir JOHN, born 1815 in Ramshorn, Glasgow, emigrated with his family to Kingston, Upper Canada, in 1820, Canada's first Prime Minister from 1867 to 1873 and from 1878 to his death in 1891. [Ramshorn church]

MCDONALD, JOHN, born 12 April 1837 in Glasgow, a student at the Ratisbon Seminary, Germany, in 1852. [RSC.I.258] [SIG.296]

MCDONALD, MALCOLM, of the Glasgow Trongate Emigration Society, with his wife and family, emigrated via Greenock aboard the David of London, master David Gemmil, bound for Quebec on 19 May 1821. [TNA.CO42.189]

MCDONALD, MARY, born 1829, daughter of John McDonald, [1785-1844], and wife of Thomas Malcolmson Dickson, [1823-1859], died in New York in 1860. [Glasgow Cathedral gravestone]

MCDOUGAL, DUNCAN, a weaver from Glasgow, who was in New York in 1809. [NRS.CS17.1.28/477]

MCDOUGALL, JOHN, of the Cathcart Emigration Society, emigrated via Greenock on board the Earl of Buckinghamshire, Captain Johnston, bound for Quebec on 29 April 1821. [TNA.CO42.189]

MCDOUGAL, PETER, master of the James and Agnes of Glasgow from Greenock to Philadelphia, Pennsylvania, in 1816. [NRS.E504.15.113]

MCDOUGALL, P. & J., calico printers in Glasgow, sederunt books 1834-1837. [NRS.CS96.4273]

MACDOUGALL, Mrs, daughter of James McQueen in Glasgow, died at Amity Hope, Tobago, on 27 January 1837. [DPCA.1813]

MCDOWALL, WILLIAM, a merchant of Ewing, May and Company, merchants, was admitted as a burgess and guilds-brother of Glasgow on 5 February 1828, as younger son of Andrew McDowall a merchant, burgess and guilds-brother. [GBR]

MCENDRICK, JAMES, of the Rutherglen Emigration Society, with his wife, emigrated via Greenock aboard the Commerce of Greenock, Captain Covendale, bound for Quebec on 11 May 1821. [TNA.CO42.189]

MCEWAN, ALEXANDER ROY, born 16 January 1828, son of James McEwan in Glasgow, was educated at Glasgow University around 1844, settled in New York in 1853, died in Brooklyn, New York, on 12 November 1860. [ANY]

MCEWAN, WILLIAM, President of the Glasgow Loyal Agricultural Emigration Society, with his wife and family, emigrated via Greenock aboard the George Canning, Captain Potter, bound for Quebec on 14 April 1821. [TNA.CO42.189]

MCEWAN, Captain, master of the Brooksby of Glasgow bound from Loch Boisdale with passengers for Quebec in 1851. [BPP]

MCEWING, JOHN, born 1774, a mariner from Glasgow, was naturalised in South Carolina on 9 February 1804. [NARA.M1183.1]

MCFADYEN, JAMES, born 3 May 1790 in Glasgow, son of John McFadyen a merchant, was educated at Glasgow University around 1813, a lecturer in Glasgow from 1822 to 1824, a physician and botanist in Jamaica until his death there on 24 November 1850. [Car.4.80][MAGU][SG.1756]

MCFARLAN, ALEXANDER, master of the George of the Clyde testament, 1811, Comm. Glasgow. [NRS]

MACFARLANE, JAMES, born 1800 in Glasgow, son of James MacFarlane, married Jean Hunter, emigrated to America in 1829, settled in the Wyoming Valley. [CMF]

MACFARLANE, PARLAN, son of Thomas MacFarlane in Pollockshaws, emigrated to America in the 1820s, an Indian trader in St Paul, Minnesota, died 1874. [CMF]

MCFIE, KENNETH, a carpenter aboard the Diana of Glasgow, testament, 1823, Comm. Glasgow. [NRS]

MCGILL, ALEXANDER, master of the Venus of Glasgow from Greenock to Newfoundland in 1814, 1815, and 1816. [NRS.E504.104/107/111]

MCGILL, THOMAS, born 1774 in Port Glasgow, a Knight of the Order of the Redeemer of Greece, Consul to Greece also to Bavaria, died in Malta on 8 October 1844. [AJ.5054] [GrAd.15.11.1844]

MCGILLIVRAY, DONALD, a labourer in Barrowfield, Glasgow, and Janet his wife and three children, bound for Canada in 1815. [TNA.CO385.2]

MCGILLIVRAY, WILLIAM, a labourer in Barrowfield, Glasgow, with his wife Isobel and six children, bound for Canada in 1815. [TNA.CO385.2]

MCGLASHAN, ADAM, a merchant in Newfoundland, in Glasgow, a sasine in 1801. [NRS.RS.Ross and Cromarty.130]

MCGOWAN, JOHN, master of the Paragon of Glasgow from Greenock to Boston, Massachusetts in 1816 and in 1817. [NRS.E504.15.113/117]

MCGREGOR, DANIEL, a shipmaster in Glasgow, 1793. [NRS.S/H]

MCGREGOR, DUNCAN, a sailor in Glasgow, 1793. [NRS.S/H]

MCGREGOR, or CAMPBELL, JOHN, a shipmaster in Glasgow, testament, 1791, Comm. Edinburgh. [NRS]

MCGREGOR, JOHN, a merchant in New York, died in Govanbank, Glasgow, in 1802. [AJ.2851]

MCGREGOR, MALCOLM, a steward aboard the SS Britannia, testament, 1820, Comm. Glasgow. [NRS]

MCGREGOR, ROBERT, a merchant of Robert McGregor and Company merchants in Brunswick Place, Glasgow, was admitted as a burgess and guilds-brother of Glasgow on 4 June 1828, as younger son of Duncan McGregor a maltman, burgess and guilds-brother. [GBR]

MCGRIGOR, ALEXANDER, of Kernock, a writer in Edinburgh, son of Malcolm McGrigor a victualler in Glasgow, was admitted as a Notary Public on 31 January 1792, died 20 December 1853. [NRS.NP2.34.321]

MCHENRY, ROBERT, born in Glasgow, died in Darien, Georgia, on 7 September 1822. [GCS.10 September 1822]

MCILHOSE, JAMES, a writer in Glasgow, later in Jamaica in 1796. [NRS.CS17.1.15/215]

MCILQUHAM, JAMES, of the Cambuslang Emigration Society, with his wife and family, emigrated via Greenock aboard the George Canning, Captain Potter, bound for Quebec on 14 April 1821. [TNA.CO42.189]

MCILQUHAM, PETER, of the Cambuslang Emigration Society, emigrated via Greenock aboard the George Canning, Captain Potter, bound for Quebec on 14 April 1821. [TNA.CO42.189]

MCILQUHAM, Reverend WILLIAM, born 1760, minister of the Church of Relief, Tollcross, Glasgow, died on 2 September 1822. [SM.90.631]

MCINDOE, ALEXANDER, a merchant in Glasgow, died 1791. [Ramshorn gravestone]

MCINDOE, JOHN, a wright of Grieve and Scott wrights, was admitted as a burgess and guilds-brother on 8 June 1827; having served his apprenticeship under Archibald Grieve and John Scott, wrights, burgesses and guild-brothers. [GBR]; a merchant in Glasgow, died 22 April 1850. [Ramshorn gravestone]

MCINNES, DUNCAN, of the Glasgow Wrights Emigration Society, with his wife and family, emigrated via Greenock aboard the George Canning, Captain Potter, bound for Quebec on 14 April 1821. [TNA.CO42.189]

MCINNES, PETER, born 1831 in Lanarkshire, arrived in Virginia in 1853, took the Oath of Allegiance on 21 May 1859. [Norfolk Circuit Court records]

MCINTOSH, DUNCAN, of the Barrowfield Road Emigration Society, with his wife and family, emigrated via Greenock aboard the George Canning, Captain Potter, bound for Quebec on 14 April 1821. [TNA.CO42.189]

MCINTOSH, JOHN, of the St John's Parish Emigration Society, with his wife, son and daughter, emigrated via Greenock aboard the Commerce of Greenock, Captain Covendale, bound for Quebec on 11 May 1821, was granted land in Dalhousie, Upper Canada, on 6 August 1821. [TNA.CO42.189] [PAO]

MACINTOSH, THOMAS, a cashier in Glasgow, father of George Morris MacIntosh a clerk in Rangoon, Burma, who died on 18 June 1881. [NRS.S/H]

MCINTYRE, DAVID, of the Kirkman Finlay Emigration Society, with his wife, and two daughters, emigrated via Greenock on board the Commerce of Greenock, Captain Coverdale, bound for Quebec on 11 May 1821, was granted land in Lanark, Upper Canada, on 27 July 1821. [TNA.CO42.89] [PAO]

MCINTYRE, JOHN, eldest son of Donald McIntyre, a craftsman at Antigua Bay, Jamaica, at Glasgow University in 1805. [MAGU]

MCINTYRE, MALCOLM, born 1791, a shoemaker, died 12 August 1877, husband of Catherine McArthur, born 1795, died 7 July 1857. [Maryhill gravestone]

MACK, HAMILTON, a farmer in Westinghouse, Carluke, died 25 October 1842, father of John Mack a farmer in Payson, Illinois. [NRS.S/H]

MACK, WILLIAM, a writer inn Airdrie, dead by 1849. [NRS.S/H]

MACKAY, HUGH, a famer and weaver in Gorbals, with Betty his wife and five children, applied to settle in Canada on 25 February 1815. [NRS.RH9] [TNA.CO385.2]

MCKAY, JAMES, a merchant from Glasgow, settled in St John, New Brunswick, died intestate on 30 January 1828, inventory, 7 September 1828, New Brunswick.

MCKAY, WILLIAM, a former soldier of the 70th Regiment of Foot, a weaver in Braidswood, Lanark, applied to settle in Canada on 13 April 1827. [TNA.CO384.5.959]

MCKEAN, ANDREW, of the Barrowfield Road Emigration Society, with his wife and family, emigrated via Greenock aboard the George Canning, Captain Potter, bound for Quebec on 14 April 1821. [TNA.CO42.189]

MCKECHNIE, JAMES, master of the Janet Dunlop of Glasgow from Greenock to Quebec in 1814, and from Greenock to Montreal in 1815 also in 1816. [NRS.E504.15.105/108/111]

MCKEICH, GRACE, fourth daughter of Peter McKeich in Port Glasgow, married Richard Johnson a merchant in Montreal, Quebec, on 4 April 1831. [AJ.4366]

MCKELLAR, DUGALD, a messenger at arms, Glasgow, 1849. [POD]

MACKENZIE, ALEXANDER, from Glasgow, a mercantile agent in Charleston, South Carolina, Nassau, and New York, around 1802. [NRS.CS238.L655]

MCKENZIE, ANDREW, a merchant in Dominica, later in Glasgow, a deed, 1792. [NRS.RD3.274.826]

MCKENZIE, ARCHIBALD, of the Abercrombie Emigration Society, with his wife and family, emigrated via Greenock aboard the David of London, master David Gemmil, bound for Quebec on 19 May 1821. [TNA.CO42.189]

MACKENZIE, EDWARD, a merchant from Glasgow, married Margaret Welch, daughter of William Welch a merchant in New York, on 27 October 1823. [DPCA.1110]

MCKENZIE, JAMES, from Blantyre, emigrated via Greenock aboard the Portaferry, bound for Quebec in May 1832. [QM.13.6.1832] [GWS]

MCKENZIE, JOHN, a baker from Port Glasgow, settled in New York by 1824. [NRS.RS4.1933]

MCKENZIE, ROBERT, son of John McKenzie a silk weave in Glasgow, was apprenticed to George Gregory, a tinplate worker in Edinburgh, for seven years on 7 January 1796. [ERA]

MCKENZIE, THOMAS, master of the Rebecca of Glasgow from Greenock to Quebec in 1816, etc. [NRS.E504.15.113, etc]

MCKERRACHER, ALEXANDER, messenger at arms, Glasgow, 1849. [POD]

MCKIE, JAMES, a tea dealer in Glasgow, a victim of forgery in 1830. [NRS.AD14.31.109]

MCKIM, ROBERT, a merchant of the firm Smith and McKim of 60 Queen Street, Glasgow, was admitted as a burgess and guilds-brother of Glasgow, on 11 February 1825, by right of his wife Jean Henderson Gilchrist, eldest daughter of William Gilchrist a cordiner, burgess and guilds-brother. [GBR]

MCKINLAY, JOHN, and his wife from Glasgow, emigrated via Greenock aboard the Portaferry, bound for Quebec in May 1832. [QM.13.6.1832][(GWS]

MCKINLAY, JOHN STEWART, born 17 April 1850 in Airdrie, emigrated with his parents to Brown County, Ohio, in 1852, settled in Philadelphia, Pennsylvania, in 1869, a lawyer there, died on 31 May 1892. [AP]

MCKINNON, DONALD, of the Bridgeton Canadian Emigration Society, with his wife and family, emigrated via Greenock aboard the George

Canning, Captain Potter, bound for Quebec on 14 April 1821. [TNA.CO42.189]

MCKINNON, JOHN, sr., of the Bridgeton Canadian Emigration Society, with his wife and family, emigrated via Greenock aboard the George Canning, Captain Potter, bound for Quebec on 14 April 1821. [TNA.CO42.189]

MCKINNON, JOHN, jr., of the Bridgeton Canadian Emigration Society, emigrated via Greenock aboard the George Canning, Captain Potter, bound for Quebec on 14 April 1821. [TNA.CO42.189]

MCKIRDY, ALEXANDER, a skipper in Port Glasgow, testament, 1805, Comm. Glasgow. [NRS]

MCLACHLAN, A., agent for the Greenock Bank in Port Glasgow in 1849. [POD]

MACLAE, HUMPHREY EWING, of Cathkin, born 19 September 1770, died 10 April 1860, husband of Jean Brown, born 15 November 1774, died 27 November 1874. [Ramshorn church crypt]

MCLAREN, JOHN, a weaver, with his wife Elizabeth Crawford, from Bridgeton, Glasgow, settled in Philadelphia, Pennsylvania, before November 1814. [NRS.CS17.1.34/26]

MCLAREN, ROBERT, President of the Glasgow Wrights Emigration Society, with his wife and family, emigrated via Greenock aboard the George Canning, Captain Potter, bound for Quebec on 14 April 1821. [TNA.CO42.189]

MCLARTY, MALCOLM, born 1845, son of Malcolm McLarty and his wife Helen Gow Thomson, died in St Croix, Danish West Indies, on 10 February 1863, [Port Glasgow gravestone]

MCLAURIN, DONALD, first son of Reverend John McLaurin in Lanarkshire, matriculated at Glasgow University in 1826, a surgeon and a justice of the peace in St Thomas in the Vale, Jamaica, died in 1842. [MAGU]

MCLAY, DAVID, of the Glasgow Union Emigration Society, emigrated via Greenock aboard the George Canning, Captain Potter, bound for Quebec on 14 April 1821. [TNA.CO42.189]

MCLAY, HUGH, of the Glasgow Union Emigration Society, wth his wife, emigrated via Greenock aboard the George Canning, Captain Potter, bound for Quebec on 14 April 1821. [TNA.CO42.189]

MACLAY, MARY, daughter of Reverend Archibald MacLay, daughter of William Brown a seedsman in Glasgow, died in New York on 20 September 1848. [SG.1765]

MACLEAN, CHARLES, a sailor from Glasgow, in America, testament, 1795, Comm. Edinburgh. [NRS]

MACLEAN, JOHN, born 1 March 1771 in Glasgow, son of John MacLean and his wife Agnes Lang, a surgeon and a chemist who was educated in Glasgow, Edinburgh, and Paris, emigrated to America in 1795, Professor of Chemistry and Natural Philosophy at Princeton University, died in Princeton, New Jersey, on 17 February 1851. [MAGU]

MCLEAN, JOHN, son of John McLean in Glasgow, was educated at Glasgow University in 1794, died at the Bay of Honduras on 14 March 1806. [MAGU]

MCLEAN, JOHN, master of the Coquette of Glasgow from Greenock to New Orleans, Louisiana, in 1816. [NRS.E504.15.111]

MCLEAN, LACHLAN, of the Brownfield and Anderston Emigration Society, emigrated via Greenock on board the Earl of Buckinghamshire, Captain Johnston, bound for Quebec on 29 April 1821, with his wife, three sons, and four daughters, was granted land in Ramsay, Upper Canada, on 26 July 1821. [TNA.CO42.189] [PAO]

MCLEAN, PATRICK, born 25 April 1807 in Gorbals, Glasgow, son of Reverend James McLean, a merchant in Buenos Ayres, Argentina, died on 3 February 1855. [F.3.1855]

MCLEAN, ROBERT CRAWFORD, born 21 August 1811 in Gorbals, Glasgow, son of Reverend James McLean, a merchant in Monte Video, Uruguay, and in Manchester, England, died on 29 April 1870. [F.3.409]

MCLEA, FREDERIC, of the Barrowfield Road Emigration Society, with his wife and family, emigrated via Greenock aboard the George Canning, Captain Potter, bound for Quebec on 14 April 1821. [TNA.CO42.189]

MCLEAN, CHARLES, a sailor from Glasgow, in America, testament, 1795, Comm. Edinburgh. [NRS]

MCLEHOSE, JAMES, in Kingston, Surry County, Jamaica, attorney for his brother William McLehose in Glasgow, deceased, appointed Claud Marshall, a writer in Glasgow, as his attorney, on 17 September 1791. [NRS.RD3.276.753]

MCLELLAN, JAMES, of the Cathcart Emigration Society, emigrated via Greenock on board the Earl of Buckinghamshire, Captain Johnston, 93 bound for Quebec on 29 April 1821, with his wife, two sons bound for Quebec on 29 April 1821, with his wife, two sons and a daughter, was granted land in Dalhousie, Upper Canada, on 21 July 1821. [TNA.CO42.189] [PAO]

MCLEHOSE, JOHN, President of the Hamilton Emigration Society, applied to settle in Canada on 7 March 1827. [TNA.CO384.5 .941]

MACLELLAN, ROBERT, in Glasgow, a deed, 20 August 1841. [NRS.RD29.3.23]

MCLELLAN, WILLIAM, President of the Cathcart Emigration Society, emigrated via Greenock on board the Earl of Buckinghamshire, Captain Johnston, bound for Quebec on 29 April 1821, with his wife, four sons and four daughters, was granted land in Lanark, Upper Canada, on 31 July 1821. [TNA.CO42.189] [PAO]

MACLELLAN, WILLIAM, son of William MacLellan, a manufacturer in Glasgow, and his wife Grace Gordon McLean, died in Montreal, Quebec, in 1864. [Glasgow Cathedral plaque]

MCLEOD, MALCOLM, a planter in St Thomas, Jamaica, appointed John Munro, a bricklayer, as his attorney, on 28 May 1803. [NRS.RD3.299.436]

MCLEOD, Reverend NORMAN, in Barony parish, Glasgow, father of Norman McLeod, born 3 October 1853, a journalist who emigrated to America, died in Chicago, Illinois, in April 1897. [F.3.394]

MCLELAND, JOHN, from Cambuslang, with his wife and children, emigrated to Canada on the Brock in 1820, was granted land in Dalhousie, Upper Canada, on 27 October 1821. [PAO]

MCLELLAND, JOHN GOURLIE, born 10 May 1850 in Glasgow, son of John McLelland and his wife Elizabeth Ann Gourlie, settled in New York by 1869. [MG]

MCLENNAN, Mrs, of the Bridgeton Transatlantic Emigration Society, with her family, emigrated via Greenock aboard the George Canning, Captain Potter, bound for Quebec on 14 April 1821. [TNA.CO42.189]

MCLEOD, JOHN, a labourer in Glasgow, and his wife Janet, were bound for Canada in 1815. [TNA.CO385.2]

MCLERAN, ARCHIBALD, born 1771 in Glasgow, a millwright who was naturalised in South Carolina on 9 November 1814. [NARA.M1183.1]

MCLEROY, WILLIAM, a merchant of the firm McLeroy and Son, muslin manufacturers at Melville Works, Craigenstock, was admitted as a burgess and guilds-brother of Glasgow on 30 August 1825, as eldest son of John Macleroy a burgess and guilds-brother, [GBR]

MCMILLAN, DONALD, born 1793, a labourer in Port Glasgow, emigrated via Port Glasgow aboard the Favourite of St John, master John Hyndman, bound for St John, New Brunswick, on 22 October 1815. [PANB.ms.RS23E.9798]

MCMILLAN, DUNCAN, from Glasgow, a farmer and weaver, was bound for Canada in 1815. [TNA.CO385.2]

MCMILLAN, HUGH, of the Bridgeton Canadian Emigration Society, with his wife and family, emigrated via Greenock aboard the George Canning, Captain Potter, bound for Quebec on 14 April 1821. [TNA.CO42.189]

MCMILLAN, P., a surgeon in Glasgow, applied to settle in Canada on 4 March 1815. [NRS.RH9]

MCMILLAN, WILLIAM, of the Cambuslang Emigration Society, with his wife and family, emigrated via Greenock aboard the George Canning, Captain Potter, bound for Quebec on 14 April 1821. [TNA.CO42.189]; settled in Dalhousie, Upper Canada, by 1822. [BPP.2.166]

MCMILLAN, WILLIAM, master of the New York of Glasgow from Glasgow with passengers to New York in 1858. [NARA.N237.183]

MCMURTIE, JAMES, of the Glasgow Loyal Agricultural Emigration Society, with his wife, emigrated via Greenock aboard the George Canning, Captain Potter, bound for Quebec on 14 April 1821. [TNA.CO42.189]

MCNAB, DAVID, born 1793, a labourer in Port Glasgow, emigrated via Port Glasgow aboard the Favourite of St John, master John Hyndman, bound for St John, New Brunswick, on 22 October 1815. [PANB.ms.RS23E.9798]

MCNAB, JOHN, a labourer in Gorbals, with his wife Isabel and four children, applied to settle in Canada in 1815. [NRS.RH9]

MCNAGHTON, MALCOLM M., second son of Finlay McNaghton a merchant in Glasgow, was drowned in the Mississippi River near St Louis, Missouri, on 26 April 1843. [SG.1228]

MCNAIR, PHILIP BARTON, born 1792, second son of James McNair of Greenfield, Glasgow, died in Madeira on 8 January 1813. [ARM] [SM.75.318]

MCNAIR, ROBERT, in Glasgow, a bond, 18 October 1841. [NRS.RD29.3.23]

MACNAIR, THOMAS MAXWELL, born 13 January 1827 in Glasgow, son of Matthew MacNair and his wife Mary Wallace, emigrated to America in 1849, a merchant in New York, died in Brooklyn, N.Y., on 26 June 1911. [ANY]

MCNAUGHT, DANIEL, a minister in Biggar, dead by 1820. [NRS.S/H]

MCNAUGHT, MARGARET, daughter of John McNaught in Glasgow, married Dr Frederick A. Webster of Yarmouth, Nova Scotia, in Halifax, N.S., on 26 April 1834. [NBC.2.5.1834]

MCNAUGHTON, JACOB, in Glasgow, applied to settle in Canada in 1815. [NRS.RH9]

MCNAUGHTON, JOHN, born 1783, a labourer in Glasgow, with his wife Margaret born 1785, and children John born 1809, Janet born 1811, and William born 1813, emigrated via Port Glasgow aboard the Favourite of

St John, master John Hyndman, bound for St John, New Brunswick, on 22 October 1815. [PANB.ms.RS23E.9798]

MCNEISH, GEORGE, of the Hamilton Emigration Society, with his family, emigrated via Greenock on board the Commerce of Greenock, Captain Coverdale, bound for Quebec on 11 May 1821. [TNA.CO42.89]

MCNISH, JOHN, master of the Caledonia of Glasgow from Greenock to Chaleur Bay, New Brunswick, in 1818. [NRS.E504.15.166]

MCPHEARSON, JOHN, President of the Cambuslang Emigration Society, with his wife and family, emigrated via Greenock aboard the George Canning, Captain Potter, bound for Quebec on 14 April 1821. [TNA.CO42.189]

MACPHERSON, DANIEL, of the Glasgow Loyal Agricultural Emigration Society, with his wife, emigrated via Greenock aboard the George Canning, Captain Potter, bound for Quebec on 14 April 1821. [TNA.CO42.189]

MCPHERSON, DONALD, a labourer in Anderston, with his wife Margaret and three children, bound for Canada in 1815. [TNA.CO385.2]

MCPHERSON, GEORGE, a mason in Westmuir, died 18 December 1839, uncle of Henry William McPherson in America. [NRS.S/H]

MCPHERSON, JOHN HYNDMAN, son of Alexander McPherson a merchant in Glasgow, a midshipman aboard the frigate Renommee, died in Gibraltar on 13 March 1808. [SM.70.477]

MCPHERSON, JOHN, of the Brownfield and Anderston Emigration Society, emigrated via Greenock on board the Earl of Buckinghamshire, Captain Johnston, to Quebec on 29 April 1821. [TNA.CO42.189]

MCPHERSON, JOHN, of the Glasgow Loyal Agricultural Emigration Society, emigrated via Greenock aboard the George Canning, Captain Potter, bound for Quebec on 14 April 1821. [TNA.CO42.189]

MCQUADE, JAMES CROZZER, an under puddler in Motherwell, was accused of theft in 1847. [NRS.AD14.47.290]

MCQUARRIE, NEIL, of the Glasgow Wrights Emigration Society, emigrated via Greenock aboard the George Canning, Captain Potter, bound for Quebec on 14 April 1821. [TNA.CO42.189]

MCQUEEN, WILLIAM, of the Bridgeton Transatlantic Emigration Society, with his wife and family, emigrated via Greenock aboard the George Canning, Captain Potter, bound for Quebec on 14 April 1821. [TNA.CO42.189]

MCQUEEN, WILLIAM, son of James McQueen in Glasgow, died in Barbados on 24 October 1836. [AJ.4640]

MCVICAR, ALEXANDER, of the Lanarkshire Emigration Society, with his wife, son and three daughters, emigrated to Canada on the Earl of Buckinghamshire, Captain Johnston, on 29 April 1821, settled in Lanark, Upper Canada, on 27 July 1821. [PAO][TNA.CO42.189]

MCVICAR, JOHN, master of the Unity of Port Glasgow from Port Glasgow to New Brunswick in 1818. [NRS.E504.28.113]

MCVICAR, JOHN, of the Lanarkshire Emigration Society, emigrated to Canada on the Earl of Buckinghamshire, Captain Johnston, on 29 April 1821, settled in Lanark, Upper Canada, on 27 July 1821. [PAO][TNA.CO42.189]

MCWHANNEL, ARCHIBALD, a hammerman in the Gallowgate, Glasgow, was admitted as a burgess of guilds-brother of Glasgow, as younger son of Edward McWhannel a wright burgess and guilds-brother on 6 June 1815. [GBR]

MCWHINNIE, JOHN, of the Barrowfield Road Emigration Society, with his wife and family, emigrated via Greenock aboard the George Canning, Captain Potter, bound for Quebec on 14 April 1821. [TNA.CO42.189]

MACHAN, JAMES, of the Cathcart Emigration Society, emigrated via Greenock on board the Earl of Buckinghamshire, Captain Johnston, bound for Quebec on 29 April 1821, with his wife, two sons and a daughter, was granted land in Dalhousie, Upper Canada, on 21 July 1821. [TNA.CO42.189] [PAO]

MAIN, JESSIE, daughter of James Main in Glasgow, married Henry A. Hart, MD, from New Brunswick, in New York on 22 July 1837. [AJ.4679]

MAIN, MARGARET, daughter of James Main in Glasgow, married Le Baron Batsford, MD, from New Brunswick, in New York on 22 July 1837. [AJ.4679]

MAINS, WILLIAM, born 1787, a labourer in Port Glasgow, with his wife Margaret born 1790, and son William born 1812, emigrated via Port Glasgow aboard the Favourite of St John, master John Hyndman, bound for St John, New Brunswick, on 22 October 1815. [PANB.ms.RS23E.9798]

MAIR, JAMES, from Hamilton, a theological student in 1815, emigrated to America, died in 1854. [UPC]

MAITLAND, GEORGE, messenger at arms, Glasgow, 1849. [POD]

MALCOLM, HUGH, sometime in Jamaica, died in Glasgow, testament, 1795, Comm. Glasgow. [NRS]

MANN, JOHN, son of John Mann a merchant in Glasgow, a writer in Glasgow, was admitted as a Notary Public on 18 June 1799. [NRS.NP2.36.275]

MARSHALL, AGNES, daughter of Robert Marshall a merchant in Glasgow, married Campbell Douglas, a gentleman from St Thomas in the East, in Hamilton on 1 July 1793. [GM.63.670]

MARSHALL, ISABELLA, born 29 July 1742 in Lanark, daughter of John Marshall and his wife Janet Hamilton, married Dr John Graham in 1765, emigrated to America in 1789, died in New York on 2 July 1814. [WA]

MARSHALL, JAMES, from Glasgow, emigrated in 1747, settled in Frederick County, Maryland, testament dated 26 October 1799. [UNC; Williams pp] [AJ.2918]

MARSHALL, THOMAS, born in Glasgow, fourth son of Robert Marshall a merchant in Glasgow, was educated at Glasgow University around 1791, manager of the Frome Estate in Jamaica, died 15 July 1802. [Car.4.17] [AJ.2857] [MAGU]

MARSHALL, WILLIAM, son of William Marshall a craftsman in Glasgow, a student at Glasgow University in 1811, later a minister in Colinsburgh, Fife, from 1823 to 1829, then in Pickersgill, New York, from 1832 to 1843, died in 1864. [MAGU]

MARTIN, ALEXANDER, a shipbuilder from Port Glasgow, emigrated to America in April 1824. [NRS.SC53.56.4]

MARTIN, Mrs ELIZABETH, born 1757 in Hamilton, widow of John Martin, died at Mount Hope, near Shelburne, Nova Scotia, on 5 May 1839. [Halifax Journal, 27.5.1839]

MARTIN, J., born 1759 in Glasgow, died in Shelbourne, Nova Scotia, on 13 May 1830. [NS.9.6.1830]

MARTIN, JAMES, in Glasgow, a deed, 8 February 1841. [NRS.RD29.3.23]

MARTIN, JOHN, master of the Martha of Glasgow from Port Glasgow to Miramachi, New Brunswick, in 1820. [NRS.E504.28.109]

MARTIN, JOHN, born 1790, ordained in Hamilton on 31 July 1821, emigrated to Halifax, Nova Scotia, in 1821, minister of St Andrew's from 1821-1865, died 22 June 1865. [HPC]

MARTIN, ROBERT, and his wife Mary Hamilton, parents of David Martin, born 1860, died in Africa on 23 April 1903. [Cambusnethan gravestone]

MARTIN, ROGER, master of the Martha of Glasgow from Port Glasgow to Miramachi, New Brunswick, in 1818. [NRS.E504.28.100/102]

MARTIN, THOMAS, found guilty of forgery in Glasgow on 18 September 1789, and was sentenced to fourteen years transportation to the colonies. [AJ.2177]

MARTIN, Captain, master of the Jamaica of Glasgow bound from Greenock with passengers for Quebec in 1851, [BPP]; master of the Susan of Glasgow bound from Glasgow with passengers to Quebec in 1854. [QM.8.7.1854]

MASON, ROBERT, of the Cambuslang Emigration Society, with his wife and family, emigrated via Greenock aboard the George Canning, Captain Potter, bound for Quebec on 14 April 1821. [TNA.CO42.189107

MATHER, ROBERT, a merchant from Glasgow, died in Hastings, Barbados, on 13 November 1838. [SG.731]

MATTHIE, ALEXANDER, of the Barrowfield Road Emigration Society, with his wife and family, emigrated via Greenock aboard the George Canning, Captain Potter, bound for Quebec on 14 April 1821. [TNA.CO42.189]

MEIKLE, GEORGE, a merchant and silk hat manufacturer in Stockwell, Glasgow, was admitted as a burgess and guilds-brother of Glasgow on 25 February 1828, as younger son of John Meikle a merchant, burgess and guilds-brother. [GBR]

MEIKLEHAM, DAVID SCOTT, MD, born 6 January 1804 in Glasgow, son of Professor William Meikleham, was educated at the Universities of Glasgow and Oxford, a physician in Paris, Havana, and New York, settled in N.Y. in 1844, died there on 20 November 1849.
[EEC.21903][AJ.5328][SG.18.1882][GM.ns33.342][ANY]

MENZIES, JAMES, born 1795, a labourer in Glasgow, emigrated via Port Glasgow aboard the Favourite of St John, master John Hyndman, bound for St John, New Brunswick, on 22 October 1815.
[PANB.ms.RS23E.9798]

MENZIES, ROBERT, of the Brownfield and Anderston Emigration Society, emigrated via Greenock on board the Earl of Buckinghamshire, Captain Johnston, bound for Quebec on 29 April 1821, was granted land in Dalhousie, Upper Canada, on 31 July 1821. [TNA.CO42.189] [PAO]

MILLEN, QUENTIN, from Glasgow, emigrated to Edenton, North Carolina, a Loyalist who moved to Nova Scotia, later a merchant in New York until his death there on 30 August 1817. [ANY]

MILLER, ALLAN, born in East Kilbride in 1754, settled in Jamaica around 1780, died in Springfield, Hanover, Jamaica, on 3 February 1826. [DPCA.1242]

MILLER, ANDREW, born 1819, from Glasgow, died on 29 May 1846, was buried in the British Cemetery, Funchal, Madeira. [ARM]

MILLER, FLORENCE or FRANCES A., born 16 January 1851 in Glasgow, died in Rome, Italy, on 12 November 1859. [Protestant Cemetery, Rome]

MILLER, FRANCIS, son of John Miller, [1777-1841], and his wife Helen Ross, [1780-1861], settled in Mexico. [Lanark gravestone]

MILLAR, JAMES, born 1793, a labourer in Glasgow, with his wife Elizabeth born 1795, emigrated via Port Glasgow aboard the Favourite of St John, master John Hyndman, bound for St John, New Brunswick, on 22 October 1815. [PANB.ms.RS23E.9798]

MILLER, JAMES, of the Rutherglen Emigration Society, with his wife, two sons, and two daughters, emigrated via Greenock aboard the Commerce of Greenock, Captain Covendale, bound for Quebec on 11 May 1821, was granted land in Lanark, Upper Canada, on 22 August 1821. [TNA.CO42.189][PAO]

MILLER, JAMES, of the Glasgow Canadian Emigration Society, with his wife and family, emigrated via Greenock aboard the George Canning, Captain Potter, bound for Quebec on 14 April 1821. [TNA.CO42.189]

MILLER, Mrs JANET, widow of Robert Miller late of Anderston, Glasgow, died in West Galway, Fulton County, New York, on 24 April 1856. [CM.20793]

MILLER, JOHN, in Glasgow, was appointed executor of David Brown in St John's, New Brunswick, on 2 March 1812. [NRS.RD5.30.133]

MILLER, JOHN, President of the North Albion Emigration Society, with his wife, three sons, and three daughters, emigrated via Greenock on board the Commerce of Greenock, Captain Coverdale, bound for Quebec on 11 May 1821, was granted land in Lanark, Upper Canada, on 21 July 1821. [TNA.CO42.89] [PAO]

MILLER, JOHN, of the Cambuslang Emigration Society, with his wife and family, emigrated via Greenock aboard the George Canning, Captain Potter, bound for Quebec on 14 April 1821. [TNA.CO42.189]

MILLER, JOHN, master of the Cherokee of Glasgow from Greenock with passengers bound for Quebec and Montreal in 1834, 1835, 1836, 1837, and 1847. [GA][QM][BPP]

MILLER, JOHN, a merchant in Glasgow, in Jamaica by 1800, returned to Glasgow by 1821. [NRS.CS18.710.15; CS17.1.40/269]

MILLER, J., master of the James Campbell of Glasgow from Glasgow to Quebec in July 1842. [GH.13.6.1842]

MILLAR, ROBERT, in Jamaica, later in Glasgow, testament, 1821, Comm. Glasgow. [NRS]

MILLER, ROBERT, from Glasgow, emigrated via Greenock aboard the Portaferry, bound for Quebec in May 1832. [QM.13.6.1832][[GWS]

MILLER, THOMAS, a merchant in Charleston, South Carolina, later in Glasgow, testament, 17 April 1823, Comm. Glasgow. [NRS]

MILLER, WILLIAM, youngest son of Reverend Thomas Miller in Lanark, died in Spanish Town, Jamaica, on 24 October 1792. [SM.54.49]

MILLER, WILLIAM, first son of John Miller a merchant in Jamaica, matriculated at Glasgow University in 1817. [MAGU]

MILLER, WILLIAM, of the Lanarkshire Emigration Society, emigrated to Canada on the Earl of Buckinghamshire, Captain Johnston, on 29 April 1821, settled in Ramsay, Upper Canada, on 31 July 1821. [PAO][TNA.CO42.189]

MILLER, WILLIAM, of the Glasgow Canadian Emigration Society, with his wife and family, emigrated via Greenock aboard the George Canning, Captain Potter, to Quebec on 14 April 1821. [TNA.CO42.189]

MILLIGAN, ARCHIBALD, was educated at Edinburgh University, minister at Airdrie from 1846 until 1851, died in Canada. [F.3.221]

MILNE, FRANCIS, formerly a merchant in Glasgow, died in Jamaica on 14 November 1814. [Kingston, Jamaica, gravestone]

MIRRILEES, Miss, in Glasgow, married James Ewing of Halifax, Nova Scotia, in Glasgow in 1816. [AR.31.8.1816]

MITCHELL, ALEXANDER, from Glasgow, married Elizabeth Gordon Cater MacFadyen, eldest daughter of James MacFadyen, MD, of Kingston, Jamaica, in East Barnet, London, on 29 April 1857. [EEC.21091]

MITCHELL, ANDREW, from Glasgow, emigrated via Liverpool bound for Montreal, Quebec, in June 1833. [SG.2.152]

MITCHELL, DAVID, born 1835 in Glasgow, son of John Mitchell a merchant, was educated at Glasgow University, a minister in Glasgow and Forfar between 1858 and 1866, later minister of the Scots Kirk in New Jersey, died there in 1905. [F.5.287]

MITCHELL, MONCRIEFF, born 2 January 1818 in Glasgow, son of Reverend John Mitchell, a merchant in New York, died in Sea Girt, New Jersey, on 10 August 1889. [ANY]

MITCHELL, WILLIAM, a merchant from Glasgow, in Philadelphia, Pennsylvania, in 1804. [NRS.CS17.23/442]

MITCHELL, ..., from Glasgow, a volunteer under Garibaldi, was killed at Capua, Italy, in 1860. [SHR.57.177]

MOFFATT, ..., born 1766 in Glasgow, died at Montego Bay, St James, Jamaica, on 18 March 1814. [Montego Bay gravestone]

MOIR, GEORGE, a merchant in Jamaica, co-owner of the Magnet of Glasgow in 1800. [NRS.CE60.11.6/18]

MOIR, WILLIAM, of the Lanarkshire Emigration Society, emigrated to Canada on the Earl of Buckinghamshire, Captain Johnston, on 29 April 1821. [TNA.CO42.189]

MONACH, ANDREW, a merchant from Glasgow, in America by 1807. [NRS.CS17.1.26/16]

MONTEATH, GEORGE CUNNINGHAM, born 1833, son of James Monteath, a writer in Glasgow, and his wife Anne Laurie Knox, died in America on 4 December 1865. [Glasgow Cathedral plaque]

MONTEITH, WILLIAM, in Glasgow, a deed, 30 June 1841. [NRS.RD29.3.23]

MONTGOMERY, WILLIAM, born 3 March 1820 at Blantyre Mill, Lanarkshire, son of James Montgomery, settled in Maine by 1837, died in Wakefield, Massachusetts, on 15 September 1805. [ANY]

MOOD, CHRISTOPHER, master of the Portland of Glasgow from Leith via Rio de Janeiro, Brazil, bound for Tasmania, Australia, on 3 December 1827, landed in Hobart, Tasmania, on 30 May 1828 and at Melbourne, Victoria, Australia, on 2 July 1828. [EEC.18102]

MOORE, JOHN, of the Barrowfield Road Emigration Society, with his wife and family, emigrated via Greenock aboard the George Canning, Captain Potter, bound for Quebec on 14 April 1821. [TNA.CO42.189]

MOODY, JOHN, born 1787 in Glasgow, emigrated to America in 1818, took the Oath of Allegiance on 21 May 1833. [Norfolk County Circuit Court Records, Virginia]

MOOR, SAMUEL, in Glasgow, applied to settle in Canada on 3 March 1815. [NRS.H9]

MORE, JOHN, of the Glasgow Loyal Agricultural Emigration Society, with his wife and family, emigrated via Greenock aboard the George Canning, Captain Potter, bound for Quebec on 14 April 1821. [TNA.CO42.189]

MORRIS, GEORGE, from Glasgow, a divinity student in 1827, later a minister in Silverspring, Pennsylvania. [AUPC]

MORRISON, ALEXANDER, of the Barrowfield Road Emigration Society, with his wife and family, emigrated via Greenock aboard the George Canning, Captain Potter, bound for Quebec on 14 April 1821. [TNA.CO42.189]

MORRISON, ARCHIBALD, a farmer in Glasgow, bound for Canada in 1815. [TNA.CO385.2]

MORRISON, DAVID, formerly a merchant in Antigua, died at Victoria Place, West Regent Street, Glasgow, on 19 November 1859. [CM.21886]

MORRISON, JAMES, from Glasgow, a grocer, was naturalised in South Carolina on 1 June 1798. [NARA.M1183.1]

MORRISON, JAMES, born 1789 in Glasgow, a student at the University of Glasgow, a minister in Nova Scotia, from 1829 to 1833, later a minister in Bermuda from 1839 until his death on 16 August 1849. [F.7.661]

MORISON, JOHN, a merchant in Tortula in the Virgin Islands, appointed James Morison, a merchant in Glasgow, as his attorney, on 18 September 1803. [NRS.RD3.303.743]

MORRISON, JOHN, born in Lanark on 29 July 1805, emigrated to Boston in 1819, settled in New York in 1820, a haberdasher there, died in NY on 23 November 1876. [ANY]

MORRISON, JOHN, of the Cathcart Emigration Society, emigrated via Greenock on board the Earl of Buckinghamshire, Captain Johnston, bound for Quebec on 29 April 1821, was granted land in Dalhousie, Upper Canada, on 31 July 1821. [TNA.CO42.189] [PAO]

MORRISON, JOHN, born 1789, residing in 27 Nicolson Street, Lawrieston, Glasgow, applied to settle in Canada in annuary 1827. [TNA.CO384.5.937]

MORRISON, WILLIAM, born 28 September 1789 in Lanark, emigrated to New York in 1821, a merchant there, died 12 February 1860. [ANY]

MORTON, PETER, formerly of Hunter, Rainey and Morton in Glasgow, died in Pittsburgh, Pennsylvania, on 1 October 1837. [SG.8.762]

MORTON, ROBERT, born 1793, a labourer in Glasgow, emigrated via Greenock on 4 September 1817 aboard the William of New York bound for N.Y., landed there on 17 October 1817. [NY Municipal Archives] [NY Commercial Advertiser]

MOSSMAN, HUGH, a Justice of the Peace in Lanark, was appointed attorney to Robert Simpson in Florida, Montgomery County, New York, on 28 July 1812. [NRS.RD5.59.545]

MOWAT, JOHN, a carpet manufacturer from Glasgow who settled in New York by 1829. [NRS.CS17.1.4.236]

MUCKART, JOHN, in Lanark, applied to settle in Canada on 27 February 1815. [NRS.RH9]

MUIR, ALEXANDER, in Strathaven, Lanarkshire, applied to settle in Canada on 27 February 1815. [NRS.RH9]

MUIR, CATHERINE, born 1811, of Muir Park, Port Glasgow, died in Madeira on 10 April 1834. [ARM]

MUIR, JOHN, a shoemaker in Cambuslang, husband of Elizabeth Cross, sister of James Cross, a merchant in Virginia, 1789. [NRS.S/H]

MUIR, JOHN, in Quebec, later in Dalserff House, testament, 1823. [NRS]

MUIR, JOHN, born 1774, died 1839, husband of Elizabeth Sibbald, born 1781, died 1838. [Ramshorn church]

MUIR, THOMAS, son of John Muir of Greenhall, Blantyre, died in Jamaica in April 1819. [AJ.3731]

MUIR, THOMAS, of the Hamilton Emigration Society, with his wife, two sons, and three daughters, emigrated via Greenock on board the Commerce of Greenock, Captain Coverdale, bound for Quebec on 11 May 1821, was granted land in Lanark, Upper Canada, on 5 September 1821. [TNA.CO42.89] [PAO]

MUNRO, DONALD, a merchant in Glasgow, was admitted as a burgess and freeman of Ayr on 12 December 1810. [ABR]

MUNRO, JOHN, of HMS Cambrian, eldest son of George Munro in Glasgow, died in Malta on 17 June 1821. [S.5.246]

MUNRO, JOHN, of the Strathaven and Kilbride Emigration Society, emigrated via Greenock aboard the George Canning, Captain Potter, bound for Quebec on 14 April 1821. [TNA.CO42.189]

MUNRO, ROBERT, a messenger at arms, Glasgow, 1849. [POD]

MURRAY, ALEXANDER, of the Glasgow Wrights Emigration Society, emigrated via Greenock aboard the George Canning, Captain Potter, bound for Quebec on 14 April 1821. [TNA.CO42.189]

MURRAY, GEORGE, son of Dr George Murray in Glasgow, was educated at Glasgow University in 1821, later was a missionary in Blenheim, Canada, died in Princeton, Ontario, on 26 April 1869. [MAGU]

MURRAY, JOHN J., late from Staten Island, New York, in Glasgow in 1805, US Consul, died in Glasgow on 4 April 1805. [GM.75.389] [NRS.CS17.1.24/164; RD4.277.37] [AJ.2987]

NIMMO, DAVID, born 1821, a miner in Forth, Carnwath, was accused of an assault with a firearm at Auchterhead, Cambusnethan, in 1849. [NRS.AD14.49.419]

NIMMO, JOHN, son of John Nimmo a tailor in Strathaven, a messenger in Strathaven, was admitted as a Notary Public on 12 June 1799. [NRS.NP2.36.277]

NISBET, ALEXANDER, a merchant, was admitted as a burgess and guilds-brother of Glasgow, on 29 November 1839, as eldest son of John Nisbet, sometime a merchant in Boston, Massachusetts, afterwards 107 in London, who was the younger son of Alexander Nisbet of Waterhead a hammerman, burgess and guilds-brother of Glasgow. [GBR]

NISBET, GEORGE, son of George Nisbet of Cairnhill, Old Monklands, was educated at Glasgow University in 1781, died in Westmoreland, Jamaica, on 30 January 1811. [MAGU][Car.4.17]

NISBET, JOHN, a merchant of the firm A. and J. Nisbet, ironmongers of 100-102 Trongate, Glasgow, was admitted as a burgess and guilds-brother of Glasgow, on 25 December 1839, as younger son of John Nisbet, sometime a merchant in Boston, Massachusetts, afterwards in London, who was the younger son of Alexander Nisbet of Waterhead a hammerman, burgess and guilds-brother of Glasgow. [GBR]

NISBET, JAMES, of the Rutherglen Emigration Society, and his wife Betty Brown, two sons, and a daughter, emigrated via Greenock aboard the Commerce of Greenock, Captain Covendale, bound for Quebec on 11 May 1821, was granted land in Sherbrook, Upper Canada, on 24 July 1821. [TNA.CO42.189] [PAO]

NISH, ANTHONY, messenger at arms, Glasgow, 1849. [POD]

NIVEN, DAVID, a writer from Glasgow, died on passage to the West Indies on 19 November 1799. [GM.70.182]

NIVEN, HUGH, born 23 August 1812, died 10 June 1880. [Ramshorn church]

NIVISON, ALEXANDER, born 7 July 1828 in Roberton, son of Reverend Alexander Nivison and his wife Christina Thomson, died in Melbourne, Victoria, Australia, in 1861. [F.2.190]

NIVISON, DAVID THOMSON, born 5 January 1834 in Roberton, son of Reverend Alexander Nivison and his wife Christina Thomson, died in Calcutta, India, on 20 August 1867. [F.2.190]

NOBLE, JOHN, born 1825, son of James Noble in Biggar, died in New York on 11 September 1879. [S.11296]

NORRIS, WILLIAM, born 1834, a butcher from Glasgow, died in Greymouth, New Zealand, on 29 September 1884. [S.12908]

NORVAL, JAMES, born 1823 in Glasgow, was educated at Glasgow University, a surgeon, settled in New York in 1850, died there on 21 May 1874. [ANY]

OGILVIE, JOHN, eldest son of John Ogilvie a glass merchant in Glasgow, died in Kingston, Jamaica, on 19 December 1830. [EEC.18608]

ORR, MATTHEW, a merchant in Glasgow, second son of William Orr of Barrowfield, emigrated to Tobago on 6 December 1778, brother of John Orr of Barrowfield, Lanarkshire, Administration, 24 December 1790 PCC. [TNA]; in Barbados, testament, 14 February 1791, Comm. Edinburgh. [NRS]

OSBORNE, JAMES, a merchant of Stewart, Pott and Osborn, wine and spirit merchants in the Old Post Office Court, Glasgow, was admitted as a burgess and guilds-brother of Glasgow on 22 October 1828. [GBR]

OUGHTERSON, Reverend ARTHUR, born 1735, died in the Manse of West Kilbride on 14 September 1822. [SM.90.632]

OWEN, DAVID DALE, born 24 June 1807 in New Lanark, son of Robert Owen and his wife Ann Dale, a geologist who emigrated to America in 1827, died at New Harmony, Indiana, on 13 November 1860. [WA]

PAGAN, JOHN, son of William Pagan a merchant in Glasgow, died in Quebec on 8 October 1799. [EA.3753.390]

PAGAN, ROBERT, born 1750 in Glasgow, arrived as a Loyalist in New Brunswick in 1783, was a member of the first House of Assembly of New Brunswick, died in St Andrews, N.B. on 23 November 1821. [CG.28.11.1821]

PAGAN, WILLIAM, a merchant on St John's Island, Nova Scotia, appointed Walter Ewing MacLean of Cathkin, James Ewing a merchant in Glasgow, Thomas Rowan of Bellahouston, John Lang a writer in Glasgow, Archibald Lang a writer in Glasgow, and Andrew Mitchell a writer in Glasgow, as his factors, 12 October 1813. [NRS.RD5.40.451]

PAGAN, WILLIAM, born 1744 in Glasgow, eldest son of William Pagan and his wife Margaret Maxwell, a merchant in New York in 1769, a Loyalist who settled as a merchant in St John, New Brunswick, in 1783, a member of the Legislature of St John, died there on 12 March 1819. [CG.24.3.1819][DCB]

PAGAN, Miss, born 1758, sister of William Pagan in St John, New Brunswick, died in Bogton, Cathcart parish, Glasgow, on 5 June 1824. [CG.9.9.1824]

PAIRMAN, ROBERT, in Biggar, was a victim of forgery and theft in 1850. [NRS.AD14,50.521]

PARK, HUGH, of the Cambuslang Emigration Society, with his wife and family, emigrated via Greenock aboard the George Canning, Captain Potter, bound for Quebec on 14 April 1821. [TNA.CO42.189]

PARK, JAMES, of the Cambuslang Emigration Society, with his wife and family, emigrated via Greenock aboard the George Canning, Captain Potter, bound for Quebec on 14 April 1821. [TNA.CO42.189]

PARKER, CHARLES STUART, born 17 June 1771 in Norfolk, Virginia, a merchant in Glasgow, died in Fairlie, Ayrshire, on 17 July 1828. [Glasgow Cathedral plaque]

PARKER, GEORGE, born 1788 in Glasgow, died in Plantin Garden, Jamaica, on 12 March 1811. [DPCA.461]

PARKER, JOHN, in Glasgow, a deed, 30 March 1841. [NRS.RD29.3.23]

PATERSON, ADAM, of the Rutherglen Emigration Society, emigrated via Greenock aboard the Commerce of Greenock, Captain Covendale, bound for Quebec on 11 May 1821. [TNA.CO42.189]

PATTERSON, or SCOTT, CHARLOTTE, was sentenced to transportation to the colonies for fourteen years, at Glasgow on 26 April 1811. [SM.83.5/393]

PATERSON, GRACE, born 1854, daughter of John Paterson and his wife Agnes Blackwood, died in Melbourne, Victoria, Australia, on 8 July 1925. [Douglas gravestone]

PATERSON, JAMES, of the Glasgow Wrights Emigration Society, with his wife and family, emigrated via Greenock aboard the George Canning, Captain Potter, bound for Quebec on 14 April 1821. [TNA.CO42.189]

PATERSON, JAMES, of the Strathaven and Kilbride Emigration Society, with his wife and family, emigrated via Greenock aboard the George Canning, Captain Potter, bound for Quebec on 14 April 1821. [TNA.CO42.189]

PATERSON, JAMES, born 1832, son of John Paterson and his wife Janet Greenshields, died in Young, New South Wales, Australia, on 4 March 1878. [Douglas gravestone]

PATERSON, JANE NICOL, born 1844, daughter of Robert Paterson in Glasgow, died on 14 March 1862 and was buries in the British Cemetery, Funchal, Madeira. [ARM]

PATERSON, JOHN, master of the Clyde of Glasgow from Greenock to Charleston, South Carolina, in 1816. [NRS.E504.15.111]

PATERSON, JOHN, and his wife Agnes Blackwood in Glentaggart, parents of Hew Blackwood Paterson, born 20 July 1851, died in Bewick, Australia, on 25 March 1925. [Douglas gravestone]

PATERSON, JOHN, a miner in Pennsylvania, son and heir of James Paterson a joiner in Glasgow who died on 20 December 1868. [NRS.S/H]

PATERSON, LILIAS, wife of J. B. Laure in Boston, Massachusetts, died at 26 Findlay Street, Glasgow, on 19 October 1849. [SG.1866]

PATERSON, SAMUEL, born 11 June 1806, son of William Paterson, was educated at Glasgow University, minister at Blantyre from 1843 until his death on 2 May 1860. [F.3.1860]

PATERSON, THOMAS B., son of Reverend Robertson in Biggar, died in Deal, England, on his return from Spain in 1809. [SM.71.880]

PATERSON, THOMAS, of the Bridgeton Transatlantic Emigration Society, emigrated via Greenock aboard the George Canning, Captain Potter, bound for Quebec on 14 April 1821. [TNA.CO42.189]

PATERSON, THOMAS GREENSHIELDS, born 1849 fifth son of Alexander Paterson of Carmicoup, Douglas, died in Montreal, Quebec, on 17 March 1874. [EC.27925]

PATERSON, WILLIAM, born 1822, from Glasgow, died on 12 February 1851, was buried in the British Cemetery, Funchal, Madeira. [ARM]

PATON, COLIN, portioner of Bothwell, 1794. [NRS.CS271.728]

PATON, ROBERT, IN THE Gorbals, applied to settle in Canada on 2 March 1815. [NRS.RH9]

PATON, R., master of the Cashmere of Glasgow from Glasgow with passengers bound for Quebec in 1849. [BPP]

PATON, ROBERT, and his wife Jean Miller [died 6 December 1869], in Glasgow, parents of Robert Paton who settled in New Zealand by 1880. [NRS.S/H]

PATON, WILLIAM, born 1779 in Lanarkshire, died in Detroit on 17 August 1849, Christine, his wife, born 1783 in Lanarkshire, died on 7 August 1849 in Detroit, Michigan. [SG.18611][W.X.1046]

PATRICK, ROBERT, from Shotts, a merchant in Bermuda, uncle of Margaret Easson, wife of Dandridge Henley in Virginia, 1823. [NRS.S/H]

PATRICK, WILLIAM, born 1771 in Kilsyth, a minister in Lockerbie, Dumfries-shire, from 1802 until 1815, then in Mergomish, Nova Scotia, from 1815 until his death on 25 November 1844. [UPC]

PATTISON, GRANVILLE SHARP, born 1791 in Glasgow, son of John Pattison in Kelvin Grove, was educated at Glasgow University, emigrated to Philadelphia in 1819, Professor of Anatomy at the University of New York, died there on 12 November 1851. [ANY] [FJ.989]

PATTISON, JAMES, a physician in Glasgow, father of James Pattison a minister in Queensland and New South Wales, Australia, after 1862. [F.4.36]

PATTON, WILLIAM, in Lanark, a former Lieutenant of the 10th Veteran Battalion, applied to settle in Canada in 1819. [TNA.CO384.5.543]

PAUL, ALEXANDER, son of Thomas Paul a banker in Lanark, a merchant, was admitted as a burgess and guilds-brother of Glasgow in 1846. [GBR]

PAUL, JAMES, President of the Glasgow Union Emigration Society, emigrated via Greenock aboard the George Canning, Captain Potter, bound for Quebec on 14 April 1821. [TNA.CO42.189]

PAUL, JOHN, born 1751 in Lanark, he fought in the American War of Independence, settled in New Brunswick, in 1783, died in St John, NB, on 29 April 1833. [Saint John Weekly Observer]

PAUL, JOHN, of the Rutherglen Emigration Society, with his wife, two sons, and four daughters, emigrated via Greenock aboard the Commerce of Greenock, Captain Covendale, bound for Quebec on 11 May 1821, was granted land in Dalhousie, Upper Canada, on 9 September 1821. [TNA.CO42.189] [PAO]

PAUL, MONTGOMERY, of the Glasgow Union Emigration Society, with his wife and family, emigrated via Greenock aboard the George Canning, Captain Potter, bound for Quebec on 14 April 1821. [TNA.CO42.189]

PAUL, THOMAS, agent in Lanark for the Commercial Bank of Scotland in 1849. [POD]

PEARSON, P., possibly from Glasgow, a volunteer under Garibaldi in Italy in 1860. [SHR.57.176]

PEAT, JOHN, son of James Peat a shoemaker in Lanark, was apprenticed to John Orr, a barber in Edinburgh, for five years, on 3 October 1793. [ERA]

PENMAN, JAMES, from South Carolina, was admitted as an honorary burgess and guilds-brother of Glasgow on 2 September 1784. [GBR]

PERCIVAL, JOHN, born 1785, a labourer in Port Glasgow, emigrated from there aboard the Favourite of St John bound for St John, New Brunswick, on 22 October 1815. [PANB.msR23E.9798]

PETER, ROBERT, born 1726 in Glasgow, son of Thomas Peter and his wife Jean Dunlop, emigrated to America around 1745, died 15 November 1806. [BAF]

PETERKIN, L., late of Glasgow, died in New York on 12 August 1803. [EEC.14321]

PETERSON, PETER, messenger at arms, Glasgow, 1849. [POD]

PETIGREW, ALEXANDER, son of John Petigrew in Glasgow, was educated at Glasgow University from 1799 until 1805, a procurator and writer in Glasgow, died in Havanna, Cuba, in October 1825. [MAGU]

PHILLIPS, MARTHA, fourth daughter of John Phillips of Stobcross, married John Reid from Clarendon, Jamaica, at Logie Green, Glasgow, on 1 February 1808. [SM.70.157]

PHYFE, DUNCAN, born 1770 in Glasgow, emigrated to America in 1783, a furniture maker in New York from 1796 until his death in 1850. [TSA]

PINKERTON, ROBERT, of the Camlachie Emigration Society, emigrated via Greenock on board the Commerce of Greenock, Captain Coverdale, bound for Quebec on 11 May 1821, was granted land in Sherbrook, Upper Canada, on 1 August 1821. [TNA.CO42.89] [PAO]

PIRRIE, WILLIAM, a hairdresser in Kirkintilloch, was accused of theft in 1847. [NRS.AD14.47.321]

POLLOCK, GRAY, born 18 June 1802 in Govan, son of Reverend John Pollock and his wife Margaret Dickson, died in Xalapa, Mexico, on 25 June 1836. [F.3.413]

POLLOCK, JAMES, of the Spring Bank Emigration Society with his wife and family, emigrated via Greenock aboard the David of London, master David Gemmill, bound for Quebec on 19 May 1821. [TNA.CO42.189]

POLLOCK, JAMES, a merchant of Bennie and Pollock wrights at the head of York Street, Glasgow, was admitted as a burgess and guilds-brother of Glasgow on 21 June 1827. [GBR]

POLLOCK, JOHN, from the Gorbals, a sailor in London in 1792. [NRS.S/H]

POLLOCK, JOHN, of Logiegreen, fifth son of Allan Pollock a merchant in Glasgow, was admitted to the Society of Writers to the Signet on 16 June 1807, died in Yancieville, Virginia, on 28 April 1817. [WS]

POLLOCK, MARGARET, daughter of Thomas Pollock a merchant in Glasgow, married George Johnson Harding, MD, of St John, New Brunswick, in Glasgow on 27 May 1830. [NBC.31.7.1830]

POLLOCK, MARGARET, from East Kilbride, married Andrew Blackburn jr., from Glasgow, in Ramsay, Upper Canada, on 11 March 1835. [GA.5075]

POLLOCK, MARGARET AIRCHISON, daughter of Reverend John Pollock in Govan, married Reverend Horatio Potter, Rector of St Peter's in Albany, New York, at Trinity Church, N.Y., on 26 September 1849. [EEC.21878] [SG.1867]

POLLOCK, ROBERT, a merchant, eldest son of Allan Pollock in George Square, Glasgow, died in Petersburg, Virginia, on 19 May 1811. [SM.73.558]

POLLOCK, ROBERT, son of Allan Pollock and his wife Janet Morris in Glasgow, a merchant in Petersburg, Virginia, in 1817, and in 1822. [NRS.CS17.1.37/89; CS17.1.43/319]

POLLOCK, THOMAS, a merchant, was admitted as a burgess and guilds-brother of Glasgow, as eldest son of William Pollock a barber burgess and guilds-brother of Glasgow on 15 April 1808. [GBR]

POLLOCK, THOMAS, master of the Louisa of Glasgow from Greenock to Charleston, South Carolina, in 1818. [NRS.E504.15.120]

POLLOCK, THOMAS, of the Spring Bank Emigration Society with his wife and family, emigrated via Greenock aboard the David of London, master David Gemmill, bound for Quebec on 19 May 1821. [TNA.CO42.189]

POLLOCK, WILLIAM, of the Bridgeton Transatlantic Emigration Society, with his wife and family, emigrated via Greenock aboard the George Canning, Captain Potter, bound for Quebec on 14 April 1821. [TNA.CO42.189]

PORTEOUS, GEORGE, second son of Reverend Dr Porteous in Glasgow, died in Spring Valley, Jamaica, on 6 December 1793. [SM.56.118] [F.3.443]

PORTEOUS, JAMES, born 25 June 1761 in Glasgow, son of Reverend William Porteous and his wife Grizel Lindsay, husband of Catherine..., a letter in 1817, died in Bonhill, Jamaica. [NRS.RD5.119.63] [F.3.443]

PORTER, MARY ANNE, daughter of Matthew Porter an accountant in Glasgow, married Archibald Falconer, a merchant in Trinidad, in Glasgow on 12 September 1837. [DPCA.1834]

POTT, GIDEON, born February 1786 in Glasgow, a merchant in New York by 1807, died there on 20 March 1843. [ANY]

POTTS, JASON, born 1777, a merchant in Glasgow, bound for New York aboard the George of New York on 12 August 1807. [TNA.PC1.3790]

PREASTLY, WILLIAM, of the Camlachie Emigration Society, emigrated via Greenock on board the Commerce of Greenock, Captain Coverdale, bound for Quebec on 11 May 1821. [TNA.CO42.89]

PRENTICE, EBENEZER, a merchant in Glasgow, was admitted as a burgess and guilds-brother of Glasgow on 27 August 1801, married Margaret Collins, daughter of Thomas Collins in St Croix, Danish West Indies, in Glasgow on 18 August 1801. [SM.63.587][GBR]

PRENTICE, THOMAS, born 1798 at Covington Mains, son of Archibald Prentice [1734-1813] and his second wife Helen [1757-1836], formerly a tenant farmer at Cleghorn Mill, died in Philadelphia, Pennsylvania, on 28 June 1823. [Covington gravestone]

PROUDFOOT, Reverend ALEXANDER, born 5 January 1831, son of Reverend James Proudfoot and his wife Janet Gibson, died in Rockhampton, Queensland, Australia, on 11 April 1873. [Coulter gravestone]

PROUDFOOT, ELIZABETH, born 6 May 1838, daughter of Reverend James Proudfoot and his wife Janet Gibson, died in Mildura, Victoria, Australia, on 17 September 1901. [Coulter gravestone]

PROUDFOOT, GEORGE, born 31 March 1837, son of Reverend James Proudfoot and his wife Janet Gibson, died in Camperdown, Australia, on 25 August 1864. [Coulter gravestone]

PROUDFOOT, MARY DICKSON, born 16 October 1829, daughter of Reverend James Proudfoot and his wife Janet Gibson, died in Mildura, Victoria, Australia, on 30 October 1900. [Coulter gravestone]

PROUDFOOT, WILLIAM, born 29 March 1784, son of George Proudfoot and his wife Janet Smith, was educated at Edinburgh University, minister at Strathaven from 1821 until his death on 26 November 1849, father of James Proudfoot who settled in Canada. [F.3.224]

PROVAN, ARCHIBALD, of the Glasgow Union Emigration Society, with his wife and family, emigrated via Greenock aboard the George Canning, Captain Potter, bound for Quebec on 14 April 1821. [TNA.CO42.189]

PROVAN, Dr MATTHEW, from Glasgow, died in Nanchez, Mississippi, on 4 October 1823. [BM.15.131]

PURDIE, ALEXANDER, baptised on 12 January 1767 son of Alexander Purdie, [1716-1772], and his wife Janet Scott, [1728-1804], in Thankerton, Covington, married Janet Lawrie in 1788, she died on 9 October 1808, he died in Syracuse, North America, on 9 October 1834. [Thankerton gravestone]

PURDIE, ROBERT, from Lanark, died on the Leogan Estate, Cornwall, Jamaica, on 31 August 1843. [SG.XI.1228] [EEC.20669]

PURDIE, WILLIAM, of the Glasgow Trongate Emigration Society, with his wife and family, emigrated via Greenock aboard the David of London, master David Gemmil, bound for Quebec on 19 May 1821. [TNA.CO42.189]

PURDIE, WILLIAM, of the Glasgow Trongate Emigration Society, emigrated via Greenock aboard the David of London, master David Gemmil, bound for Quebec on 19 May 1821. [TNA.CO42.189]

PURDON, ROBERT, of the Glasgow Canadian Emigration Society, with his wife and family, emigrated via Greenock aboard the George Canning, Captain Potter, bound for Quebec on 14 April 1821. [TNA.CO42.189]

QUIG, MICHAEL, born 1796 in Glasgow, a bleacher who emigrated via Londonderry to the USA, was naturalised in New York on 16 April 1821. [NARA]

RAITT, CHARLES BAILLIE, of Carphin, died in India on 31 August 1840, inventory, 1841, Edinburgh. [NRS]

RAMSAY, HUGH, master of the Venus of Glasgow from Greenock to Newfoundland in 1817, and 1818. [NRS.E504.15115/120]

RAMSAY, WILLIAM HAMILTON, a Captain of the 1st Royal Lanark Militia, married Fanny Scarth, eldest daughter of Thomas Scarth, at the British Embassy, in Dresden, Germany, on 27 August 1857. [W.XVIII.1902] 116

RAMSAY, ……., a weaver from Glasgow, settled in North Sherbrook township, Upper Canada, around 1821. [BPP.2.167]

RANKEN, Reverend ALEXANDER, born 1785, minister of Ramshorn and St David's, died 1827. [Ramshorn church]

RANKIN, ALEXANDER, master of the Caesar of Glasgow from Greenock to Pictou, Nova Scotia, in 1818. [NRS.E504.15.122]

RANKEN, ALEXANDER, born 7 March 1813 in Glasgow, son of Alexander Ranken a merchant, was educated at Glasgow University, emigrated to New York as a merchant in 1841, died in Guernsey, the Channel Islands, on 17 April 1887. [ANY]

RANKIN, ALEXANDER, a small ware merchant of 125 Trongate, Glasgow, was admitted as a burgess and guilds-brother of Glasgow on 2 September 1828, as eldest son of Alexander Rankin a mason, burgess and guilds-brother. [GBR]

RANKIN, ARCHIBALD, of the Glasgow Trongate Emigration Society, with his wife, emigrated via Greenock aboard the David of London, master David Gemmil, bound for Quebec on 19 May 1821. [TNA.CO42.189]

RANKIN, JAMES, in Hopetoun, St James, Jamaica, son of Alexander Rankin of Coustoun, subscribed to a deed in favour of James Keay and Robert Bogle, merchants in Glasgow, on 25 February 1813. [NRS.RD5.27.45]

RANKEN, JAMES, born 1815, a tobacconist, died 20 October 1903. [Ramshorn church crypt]

RANKEN, JAMES, of Ardnackaig, born 1811, died 29 October 1903. [Ramshorn church]

RANKIN, JANET, wife of J. Hyndman in America, niece and heir of Richard Kirkland, a weaver in Airdrie, who died on 30 December 1812. [NRS.S/H]

RANKINE, JOHN, a merchant in Montreal, Quebec, son of .... Rankine a surgeon in Douglas, died in Quebec in 1813. [EA.5165.13]

RANKIN, ROBERT, from Glasgow, emigrated via Greenock aboard the Portaferry, bound for Quebec in May 1832. [QM.13.6.1832][[GWS]

RANKIN, WILLIAM, in Kirk Street, Calton, Glasgow, an army pensioner, applied to settle in Canada on 16 August 1819. [TNA.CO384.5.729]

RATTRAY, ROBERT, a hatmaker from Glasgow, seventh son of James Rattray in Coupar, Angus, Perthshire, died in Cincinatti, Ohio, on 14 February 1849. [SG.1809]

RAYSIDE, WILLIAM, master of the Cherub of Glasgow from Greenock to Montreal, Quebec, in 1819. [NRS.E504.15.125]; master of the Montreal of Glasgow from Greenock to Quebec in 1816. [NRS.E504.15.111]

REDDIE, GEORGE BURD, born 21 April 1809, son of James Reddie and his wife Charlotte Marion Campbell, a Major General of the 29th Bengal Native Infantry, died in Bath on 17 March 1880. [BA.3.621]

REDDOCH, NEWTON BURGES, born 5 April 1845, son of Allan and Janet Reddoch in Laurel Bank, Shawlands, Glasgow, died in Lisbon, Portugal, on 29 March 1874. [English Cemetery, Lisbon]

REDMOND, CHRISTINA FISHER, daughter of Thomas Redmond in Philadelphia, Pennsylvania, died in Glasgow on 23 March 1844. [W.V.447]

REID, ALEXANDER, a farmer in Possill, testaments, 1795, 1796, 1798, Comm. Glasgow. [NRS]

REID, GEORGE, with his wife, and three children, from Glasgow, emigrated via Greenock aboard the Portaferry, bound for Quebec in May 1832. [QM.13.6.1832] [GWS]

REID, DANIEL, from Glasgow, declared his intention to naturalise in the East District Court, Virginia, on 28 June 1855.

REID, DAVID, master of the Trelawney testament, 1819, Comm. Glasgow. [NRS]

REID, HELENA, daughter of William Reid in Greenwich, married James Reid from Jamaica, in Glasgow on 31 March 1807. [SM.69.316]

REID, JAMES, formerly in Newton of Campsie, later in Calton of Glasgow, testament, 1800, Comm. Glasgow. [NRS]

REID, JANE, eldest daughter of William Reid a merchant in Glasgow, married Robert Smith of Mountblow, Jamaica, in Drumoyne House on 23 January 1809. [SM.71.157]

REID, JANET, spouse of William Miller a shoemaker in Glasgow, testament, 1794, Comm. Glasgow. [NRS]

REID, JANET, wife of Charles Weldon in New York, niece and heir to Jean Reid in Port Glasgow, 1857; also, daughter and heir of John Reid, a merchant from Port Glasgow, later in New York on 5 November 1857. [NRS.S/H]

REID, JOHN, from Claredon, Jamaica, married Martha Phillips, fourth daughter of John Phillips of Stobcross, in Logiegreen, Glasgow on 1 February 1808. [SM.70.157]

REID, JOHN, of the Cambuslang Emigration Society, with his wife and family, emigrated via Greenock aboard the George Canning, Captain Potter, bound for Quebec on 14 April 1821. [TNA.CO42.189]

REID, MARGARET, daughter of John Reid a grocer in Glasgow, testament, 1794, Comm. Glasgow. [NRS]

REID, MARGARET, from Glasgow, was buried in the British Cemetery, Funchal, Madeira, on 25 March 1858. [ARM]

REID, MARY, wife of John Kerr in New York, daughter and heir of John Reid a merchant from Port Glasgow, later in New York, also, heir to her aunt Jean Reid in Port Glasgow, 1857. [NRS.S/H]

REID, Dr THOMAS, Professor of Moral Philosophy at Glasgow University, testament, 1797, Comm. Glasgow. [NRS]

REID, THOMAS, of the Hamilton Emigration Society, with his family, emigrated via Greenock on board the Commerce of Greenock, Captain Coverdale, bound for Quebec on 11 May 1821, was granted land in Dalhousie, Upper Canada, on 19 July 1821. [TNA.CO42.89] [PAO]

REID, WALTER, a shipmaster in Port Glasgow, testament, 1797, Comm. Glasgow. [NRS]

REID, WILLIAM, son of Dr Andrew Reid, 95 South Portland Street, Glasgow, died at Montego Bay, Jamaica, on 15 December 1841. [GSP.705]

RENAUD, EDWARD, in Washington, grandson and heir of John Craig a merchant in Glasgow, 1865. [NRS.S/H]

RENFREW, JOHN, a merchant of 18 Brunswick Place, Glasgow, was admitted as a burgess and guilds-brother of Glasgow on 10 July 1823 as eldest son of John Renfrew, a merchant in Paisley, Renfrewshire, who was eldest son of John Renfrew a merchant there, a burgess and guilds-brother. [GBR]

RENFREW, JOHN, in Greentown, Pennsylvania, heir to his nephew Robert Renfrew a smith in Pollockshaws, Glasgow, 1837. [NRS.S/H]

RENNISON, LEWIS WILLIAMS, born 4 April 1845 in Glasgow, son of Reverend Alexander Rennison, was educated at Glasgow University, a minister in Suva, Fiji, in 1880s, died in Australia. [F.6.602]

RENWICK, ALEXANDER, first son of William Renwick a merchant in Jamaica, matriculated at Glasgow University in 1811. [MAGU]

RENWICK, JOHN, second son of William Renwick a merchant in Jamaica, matriculated at Glasgow University in 1819. [MAGU]

RICHARDSON, GEORGE, of the Glasgow-Ohio Company, settled in Ohio in 1823. [SHR.63.55]

RICHARDSON, JAMES, formerly a merchant in Glasgow, died in New York on 2 September 1799. [EA.3736.255]

RICHMOND, THOMAS, from Glasgow, died in Lisbon, Portugal, on 2 January 1852. [FJ.995] [AJ.2703]

RIDDELL, JOHN, of the Strathaven and Kilbride Emigration Society, emigrated via Greenock aboard the George Canning, Captain Potter, bound for Quebec on 14 April 1821. [TNA.CO42.189]

RIDDELL, JOHN, in Canada West, brother and heir to Robert Riddell, a tea dealer in Glasgow, who died 19 October 1858. [NRS.S/H]

RIDDELL, JOHN, a builder in York, Canada, heir of Alexander Brownlee Hamilton, a mason in Strathaven, who died 5 August 1866. [NRS.S/H]

RIDDELL, MATTHEW, from Glasgow, married Agnes Traquair Rutherford, eldest daughter of Andrew Rutherford in Toronto, Ontario, Canada, there on 4 September 1873. [GH.10523]

RIDDOCH, JOHN, brother of George Riddoch a writer in Glasgow, settled in Jamaica for thirty years, died there on 23 December 1801. [SM.64.182]

RITCHIE, AGNES, daughter of Alexander Ritchie in Glasgow and wife of Dr M. H. Haig, died in Charleston, South Carolina, on 23 November 1817. [DPCA.809]

RITCHIE, ARCHIBALD, in Reigate, Vermont, brother and heir of John Ritchie a shoemaker from Port Glasgow, in Boroondara, Victoria, Australia, who died 22 March 1860. [NRS.S/H]

RITCHIE, JAMES, son of James Ritchie a mason in Glasgow, was apprenticed to James Sibbald, a locksmith in Edinburgh, for six years, on 3 August 1795. [ERA]

RITCHIE, JAMES, master of the Neptune of Port Glasgow from Greenock to Quebec on 2 March 1815. [NRS.E504.15.107]

RITCHIE, JAMES, in Glasgow, master of the sloop Clyde, testament, 1822, Comm. Glasgow. [NRS]

RITCHIE, JOHN, a skipper in Port Glasgow, testament, 1818, Comm. Glasgow. [NRS]

RITCHIE, WILLIAM ALEXANDER, in Lancaster, USA, heir to his grand-uncle John Ritchie a merchant in Govan, also, heir to his cousins Alexander Ritchie and John Ritchie in Govan, 1842. [NRS.S/H]

RITCHIE, Captain, master of the Carolina of Port Glasgow from the River Clyde to North Carolina in 1792 and in 1793. [GM.19.9.1793]

ROBB, EDMUND BOYD, in New Brunswick, heir to his uncle William Robb a clerk in Glasgow, 1862. [NRS.S/H]

ROBB, JAMES, born 1792, died 1842, husband of Elizabeth Hutchison, born 1796, died 1879. [Ramshorn church]

ROBB, JAMES, in King's College, New Brunswick, heir to his uncle William Robb a clerk in Glasgow, 1862. [NRS.S/H]

ROBERTON, JOHN, born 1819 in Lanarkshire, son of James Roberton, a whisky importer in New York until 1872, died in Oban, Argyll, on 18 December 1882. [ANY]

ROBERTON, JOHN, a messenger at arms, Glasgow, 1849. [POD]

ROBERTS, ALLEN, in Airdrie, brother and heir of James Roberts a carter in Craig later in America, 1840. [NRS.S/H]

ROBERTS, WILLIAM, born 1775, a banker in Glasgow, died 14 April 1832. [Ramshorn church crypt]

ROBERTSON, ALEXANDER, born 1791 in Glasgow, a Hudson Bay Company employee from 1811 to 1845. [HBRS]

ROBERTSON, ANTHONY, a saddler in Patterson, New Jersey, son and heir of George Robertson in Biggar, who died 5 September 1847. [NRS.S/H]

ROBERTSON, DAVID, a merchant of Robertson and Atkinson booksellers in Trongate, Glasgow, was admitted as a burgess and guilds-brother of Glasgow on 22 August 1828, by right of his wife Frances Aitken a mason, burgess and guilds-brother. [GBR]

ROBERTSON, GEORGE, a tanner from Glasgow, settled in Virginia by 1794. [NRS.CS17.1.13/10]

ROBERTSON, GEORGE, in Biggar, died 5 September 1847, father of Anthony Robertson a saddler in Patterson, New Jersey. [NRS.S/H.1866]

ROBERTSON, HUGH, and Son, yarn merchants in Motherwell, 1792. [NRS.CS233.SEQN/R1.9]

ROBERTSON, JAMES, eldest son of Patrick Robertson a writer in Glasgow, was admitted to the Society of Writers to the Signet on 26 June 1789, died in Jamaica in April 1794. [WS]

ROBERTSON, JAMES, a skipper in Port Glasgow, master of the Aurora of Greenock, testament, 1806, Comm. Glasgow. [NRS]

ROBERTSON, JAMES, of the Glasgow Trongate Emigration Society, with his wife and family, emigrated via Greenock aboard the David of London, master David Gemmil, bound for Quebec on 19 May 1821. [TNA.CO42.189]

ROBERTSON, JAMES, from Glasgow, emigrated via Greenock aboard the Portaferry, bound for Quebec in May 1832. [QM.13.6.1832] [GWS]

ROBERTSON, JAMES, from Glasgow, emigrated via Liverpool to Montreal, Canada, in June 1833. [SG.2.1.162]

ROBERTSON, JOHN, son of John Robertson a cooper in Glasgow, a seaman aboard the Dolphin of Philadelphia, Captain O'Brian, was imprisoned in Algiers in 1785, there in July 1790. [AJ.2230]

ROBERTSON, JOHN, born 1768 in Hamilton, son of William Robertson a farmer, was educated at Glasgow University, minister at Cambuslang from 1797 until his death on 2 February 1843. [F.3.238]

ROBERTSON, JOHN, of the Abercrombie Emigration Society, with his wife and family, emigrated via Greenock aboard the David of London, master David Gemmil, bound for Quebec on 19 May 1821. [TNA.CO42.189]

ROBERTSON, JOHN, in Belton, Bell County, Texas, son and heir to Johnston Robertson, watchman at the Govan Silk Factory, Glasgow, who died 23 March 1864. [NRS.S/H]

ROBERTSON, JOHN, a joiner in San Francisco, California, son and heir of John Robertson a gardener in Govan, Glasgow, who died 9 September 1845. [NRS.S/H]

ROBERTSON, WILLIAM, a cloth lapper in Glasgow, 1819. [Ramshorn gravestone]

ROBERTSON, WILLIAM, of the Camlachie Emigration Society, with his family, emigrated via Greenock on board the Commerce of Greenock, Captain Coverdale, bound for Quebec on 11 May 1821, was granted land in Lanark, Upper Canada, on 27 July 1821. [TNA.CO42.89] [PAO]

ROBERTSON, WILLIAM, of the Govan Emigration Society, with his wife, three sons, and two daughters, emigrated via Greenock on board the Commerce of Greenock, Captain Coverdale, bound for Quebec on 11 May 1821, was granted land in Lanark, Upper Canada, on 26 July 1821. [TNA.CO42.89] [PAO]

ROBERTSON, WILLIAM, born 1834, son of William Robertson a merchant in Glasgow, a missionary in Demerara from 1872 to 1876, later a minister in Kemmingford, Quebec, from 1877 until his death on 4 January 1894. [F.3.371]

RODGER, JAMES, born 1745, a merchant in Glasgow, died 7 October 1834. [Ramshorn gravestone]

RODGER, WILLIAM, a Magistrate of Glasgow, was admitted as a burgess and guilds-brother of Ayr on 27 January 1812. [ABR]

RODGER, WILLIAM, agent of the Western Bank of Scotland in Wishaw in 1849. [POD]

ROGERS, JAMES, a wright in Hamilton, Lanarkshire, who died in August 1851, father of James Rogers a physician in St Petersburg, Russia. [NRS.S/H]

ROLLO, JAMES, of the Glasgow Trongate Emigration Society, with his wife and family, emigrated via Greenock aboard the David of London, master David Gemmil, bound for Quebec on 19 May 1821. [TNA.CO42.189]

ROSE, JAMES, master of the Waverley of Glasgow from Glasgow with passengers bound for Port Philip and Melbourne, Australia, in July 1853, landed there in November 1853. [LCL.4237/4275]

ROSS, D., master of the Elephanta of Glasgow, bound from Greenock to Quebec in July 1842. [GH.13.6.1842]

ROSS, JOHN, a merchant, was admitted as a burgess and guilds-brother of Glasgow, on 14 May 1808. [GBR]

ROSS, JOHN, born 28 June 1799, second son of Richard Ross, graduated MA from Glasgow University in 1819, a missionary in Kaffraria, South Africa, from 1823, married Helen Blair, died in King William's Town, Cape of Good Hope, South Africa, on 7 June 1878. [F.7.564]

ROSS, JOHN, a merchant in Glasgow, married Ann McKail, daughter of Angus McKail of Prospect, Montego Bay, Jamaica, in Campbelltown, Argyll, on 1 November 1824. [S.504.802]

ROSS, ROBERT, and his wife, from Glasgow, emigrated via Greenock aboard the Portaferry, bound for Quebec in May 1832. [QM.13.6.1832][GWS]

ROSS, PHILIP SIMPSON, a merchant in Montreal, Quebec, son and heir of Philip Ross in Port Dundas, Glasgow, 1859. [NRS.S/H]

ROSS, ROBERT K., in Coatbridge, a petition for sequestration in 1847. [NRS.CS279.2187]

ROSS, Mrs T., born 1795, died in Quebec on 4 December 1856. [Carluke gravestone]

ROSS, WILLIAM, was accused of neglect of duty at Hector's Bridge Cutting, Crawford, trial papers, 1848. [NRS.JC26.1848.430]

ROSS, Mrs, with her children, from Glasgow, emigrated via Liverpool to New York on 20 June 1833. [SG.153]

ROWAND, ANDREW, from Glasgow, died in Kingston, Jamaica, on 18 April 1806. [SM.68.565]

ROXBURGH, ARCHIBALD, born 1823, from Glasgow, died 20 March 1870, was buried in the British Cemetery, Funchal, Madeira. [ARM]

RUSSELL, ALEXANDER, an auctioneer and builder in Glasgow, also a bankrupt, emigrated to North America in 1826. [NRS.CS238.C18.37]

RUSSELL, JAMES, born 1805 in Lanarkshire, took the Oath of Allegiance in Norfolk Borough Court, Virginia, on 26 August 1833. [NARA]

RUSSEL, JAMES, born 3 August 1815, was educated at the Ratisbon Seminary in Germany, died in Glasgow in 1837. [SIG.295][RSC.I.1889]

RUSSELL, JAMES, a partner in the firm Ferguson and Company, cotton spinners and power loom cloth manufacturers in Glasgow, a bankrupt in 1848. [NRS.CS280.34.68]

RUSSELL, THOMAS, born 1817, son of John Russell, [1738-1867], and his wife Jane Cuthbertson, [1776-1848], a bookbinder in Trinidad, died on 28 May 1838. [Lanark gravestone]

RUSSELL, WILLIAM, born 28 April 1798, son of Alexander Russell in Glasgow, was educated at Glasgow University in 1811, emigrated to Savanna, Georgia, in 1819, Head Teacher of Chatham Academy, a teacher in Massachusetts, died in Lancaster, Massachusetts, on 17 May 1873. [MAGU]

RUTHERFORD, WILLIAM, of the Camlachie Emigration Society, with his wife, son, and daughter, emigrated via Greenock on board the Commerce of Greenock, Captain Coverdale, bound for Quebec on 11 May 1821, was granted land in Sherbrook, Upper Canada, on 1 August 1821. [TNA.CO42.89] [PAO]

RUTHERGLEN, ANDREW, a bookseller and stationer in Glasgow, sequestration, 1846. [NRS.CS280.72]

RUTHVEN, ROBERT, President of the Spring Bank Emigration Society with his wife and family, emigrated via Greenock aboard the David of London, master David Gemmill, bound for Quebec on 19 May 1821. [TNA.CO42.189]

RYBURN, THOMAS, in Jamaica, co-owner of Glasgow registered ships in 1798, died in Kingston, Jamaica, on 3 September 1799. [AJ.2707] [NRS.CE60.11.5/71/108]

SALMOND, DUNCAN, son of James Salmond in Inveraray, Argyll, a merchant who was admitted as a burgess and guilds-brother of Glasgow in 1845. [GBR]

SANDERS, JOHN, born 1772 in Glasgow, a merchant who was naturalised in South Carolina on 16 May 1805. [NARA.M1183.1]

SAWERS, WILLIAM, born 1779, son of Robert Sawers of Drumtack, East Monkland, died on Sullivan's Island, America, on 30 August 1800. [GC.1426]

SCOTT, CHARLES, a merchant from Glasgow, died in Nassau, New Providence in the Bahamas, on 18 October 1802. [EA.4050] [AJ.2867]

SCOTT, DAVID, born 17 July 1794 in Glasgow, was educated at Theology Hall in 1820, emigrated to America in 1829, a minister in Albany and in Rochester, New York, died there on 29 March 1871. ['Relief Presbyterian Church in Scotland', p.163]

SCOTT, GAVIN, from Glasgow, a hairdresser in Chatham County, Georgia, probate, 3 February 1812, Chatham County, Georgia.

SCOTT, GEORGE, son of Thomas Scott a merchant in Glasgow, died at Roaring River, Jamaica, on 15 August 1798. [GC.1123] [EA.3639]

SCOTT, GEORGE, a cartwright in Jamaica Street, Glasgow, was admitted as a burgess and guilds-brother of Glasgow on 20 December 1815. [GBR]

SCOTT, HENRIETTA, born 1786, from Glasgow, wife of Thomas Muir of Muirpark, died on 8 December 1844, was buried in the British Cemetery, Funchal, Madeira. [ARM]

SCOTT, JAMES, a merchant in New York in 1806, son of George Scott a coachmaker in Glasgow. [NRS.CS17.1.25/455, 492]

SCOTT, JAMES of the Hamilton Emigration Society, emigrated via Greenock on board the Commerce of Greenock, Captain Coverdale, bound for Quebec on 11 May 1821. [TNA.CO42.89]

SCOTT, JANET, born 1787 son of Allan Scott in Glasgow, died in Jamaica on 4 January 1819. [Kingston Cathedral gravestone, Jamaica]

SCOTT, JOHN, son of Gavin Scott, a farmer in Auchenglen, Lanarkshire, died in St Martin, Dutch West Indies, on 24 March 1807. [SM.69.477]

SCOTT, JOHN, born 1775, son of Robert Scott a banker in Glasgow, died in Jamaica on 26 October 1815. [Kingston Cathedral gravestone, Jamaica]

SCOTT, JOHN, from Glasgow, died at the Cottage, Falmouth, Jamaica, on 1 January 1851. [W.1191]

SCOTT, MARGARET, daughter of James Scott a merchant in Glasgow, and wife of James Taylor a merchant in New York, died on 19 November 1797. [AJ.2609]

SCOTT, MICHAEL, born 30 October 1789 at Cowlairs House, fifth son of Allan Scott a merchant in Glasgow, matriculated at Glasgow University in 1801, a writer and merchant in Jamaica from 1806 until 1822, died in Glasgow on 6 November 1835. [Glasgow Necropolis gravestone] [MAGU] [NRS.RD5.193.513]

SCOTT, PETER, master of the Janet Dunlop of Glasgow from Greenock to Boston, Massachusetts, in 1817, and from Greenock to Newfoundland in 1818. [NRS.E504.15.114/119]

SCOTT, REBECCA, widow of Adam Scott in Jamaica, heir to her grand father Alexander Campbell a merchant in Glasgow, 1817. [NRS.S/H]

SCOTT, ROBERT, born 1773 in Biggar, a saddler in Edinburgh, emigrated with his wife Marion Young born 1785, and children Alice born 1803, James born 1810, Robert born 1812, John born 1813, Margaret born 1816, to Canada in 1818. [TNA.CO384.3]

SCOTT, ROBERT, of the Cambuslang Emigration Society, with his wife and family, emigrated via Greenock aboard the George Canning, Captain Potter, bound for Quebec on 14 April 1821. [TNA.CO42.189]

SCOTT, WILLIAM, born 1793 in Lanarkshire, died at Red Head, St John, New Brunswick, on 9 August 1839. [NBC, 10.8.1839]

SCOTT, WILLIAM, born 1807 in Bellshill, a saddler who died in Jamaica on 30 November 1838. [Scots cemetery gravestone, Kingston, Jamaica]

SCOTT, Captain, master of the Margaret of Port Glasgow from Port Glasgow with passengers bound for Canada in 1843. [GA.5931]

SCOTT, Captain, master of the Perthshire of Glasgow from Loch Boisdale with passengers bound for Quebec in 1851. [BPP]

SCOULLAR, ANDREW, in Lanark, father of Annie Scoullar who married Henry T. Partelow a merchant in St John, New Brunswick, on 6 October 1830. [New Brunswick Courier, 9.1.1830]

SCOULLAR, GEORGE, from Lanark, married Theodosia Sayre, fourth daughter of James Sayre in Dorchester Island, New Brunswick, there on 12 November 1831. [New Brunswick Courier, 19.11.1831]

SCOULAR, JOHN, from Glasgow, emigrated via Greenock aboard the Portaferry, bound for Quebec in May 1832. [QM.13.6.1832] [GWS]

SCOULAR, MARY, born 1814 in East Kilbride, wife of Robert Pettigrew, died in Innerkip, Ontario, on 28 May 1875. [EC.28316]

SCRIVENER, B., possibly from Glasgow, served under Garibaldi in Italy in 1860. [SHR.57.176]

SEMPLE, JOHN, son of Robert Semple in Greenhead, Glasgow, died on St Thomas, Danish West Indies, in 1818. [S.69.18]

SEMPLE, ROBERT, son of Robert Semple in Greenhead, Glasgow, Governor in Chief of Rupert's Land, Hudson Bay, died in 1816. [DPCA] [SM.78.960]

SEMPLE, ROBERT, from Demerara, married Adriana Moore, daughter of William Moore in St Eustatius, Dutch West Indies, in Glasgow on 30 September 1817. [BM.2.126]

SEMPLE, ROBERT, died 1 March 1827. [Ramshorn gravestone]

SENIOR, JOSHUA, a merchant, was admitted as a burgess and guildsbrother of Glasgow on 11 January 1796, by the right of his wife Isobel Dick, daughter of Alexander Dick a merchant burgess and guildsbrother. [GBR]

SENIOR, RICHARD, son of Joshua Senior in Sandyford, Glasgow, died in New York in 1854. [S.18.10.1854]

SERVICE, JAMES, master of the Mary Ann of Port Glasgow from Greenock to New York in 1815. [NRS.E504.15.107]

SHANKS, DAVID, born 1801, son of William Shanks in Hartlop, New Monklands, was educated at Glasgow University in 1820, minister of St Andrew's, Valcartier, Quebec, died on 12 November 1871. [MAGU]

SHANKS, JOHN, in Roundknowe, Bothwell, was accused of uttering a forged bill of exchange in 1848. [NRS.AD14.48.84]

SHARP, Captain, master of the Elizabeth of Glasgow, from Glasgow to Melbourne, Victoria, Australia, in April 1853, landed there on 17 November 1853. [LCL.4189/4275]

SHAW, JESSIE, in New Brunswick, heir to George Shaw a minister in Hamilton, 1858. [NRS.S/H]

SHAW, JOHN, a ship's carpenter aboard the Hunter of Port Glasgow, died in Grenada on 21 August 1794, testament, 1795, Comm. Edinburgh. [NRS]

SHAW, JOHN, from Glasgow, later of Johnson and Company in Honduras, died in Havannah, Cuba, on 6 April 1844. [W.5.472]

SHAW, MARGARET, in New Brunswick, heir to George Shaw a minister in Hamilton, 1858. [NRS.S/H]

SHAW, MARY, in New Brunswick, heir to George Shaw a minister in Hamilton, 1858. [NRS.S/H]

SHAW, REBECCA, in New Brunswick, heir to George Shaw a minister in Hamilton, 1858. [NRS.S/H]

SHEARER, Mrs JANE, born 1816 in Hamilton, wife of Thomas Shearer in St John, New Brunswick, died at Johnston, Queen's County, N.B., on 20 January 1843. [New Brunswick Courier, 4.2.1843]

SHEDDEN, ..., born 1811, second daughter of Thomas Shedden in Glasgow, wife of Charles Jacks a Lieutenant of the US Navy, died in Middleton, Connecticut, on 9 July 1833. [SG.185]

SHERIFF, JOHN BELL, son of George Sheriff in St Petersburg, Russia, a merchant, was admitted as a burgess and guilds-brother of Glasgow on 26 September 1845. [GBR]

SHERIFF, ROBERT, son of Robert Sheriff a merchant in Glasgow, was educated at the University of Glasgow around 1819, a merchant in New York, died on Diamond Estate, St Croix, Danish West Indies, on 18 August 1847, testament, 1859. [NRS][ANY]

SHERON, WILLIAM, a skipper in Port Glasgow, testament, 1790, Comm. Glasgow. [NRS]

SHIELS, THOMAS, in Glasgow, a disposition, 15 June 1841. [NRS.RD29.3.23]

SHORTRIDGE, JOHN, born 1786, first son of William Shortridge a merchant in Glasgow, matriculated at Glasgow University in 1799, sometime in Jamaica, died London on 22 November 1878. [MAGU]

SIM, ROBERT, of the Rutherglen Emigration Society, emigrated via Greenock aboard the Commerce of Greenock, Captain Covendale, bound for Quebec on 11 May 1821, was granted land in Sherbrook, Upper Canada on 7 August 1821. [TNA.CO42.189][PAO]

SIMPSON, ROBERT, from Rothes, settled in Florida, Montgomery County, New York, appointed Hugh Mossman in Lanark, as his attorney on 28 July 1812. [NRS.RD5.59.545]

SIMPSON, Captain WALTER, of the brig Forth, died in Glasgow on 21 May 1829. [NBC.1.8.1829]

SINCLAIR, HUGH, of the Barrowfield Road Emigration Society, with his wife and family, emigrated via Greenock aboard the George Canning, Captain Potter, bound for Quebec on 14 April 1821. [TNA.CO42.189]

SINCLAIR, JAMES, possibly from Glasgow, a volunteer under Garibaldi in Italy in 1860. [SHR.57.176]

SINCLAIR, JOHN, a baker from Glasgow, died at Montego Bay, Jamaica, on 31 August 1843. [SG.XI.1239]

SLEIGH, WILLIAM, son of Douglas Sleigh in Douglas, Lanarkshire, a merchant of the Yarn Warehouse, 84 Wilson Street, Glasgow, was admitted as a burgess and guilds-brother of Glasgow on 10 February 1829. [GBR]

SMALL, JOHN, born 1732 in Kilbride near Glasgow, to America as a soldier of the 77th [Montgomery's] Regiment in 1757, fought at the Battle of the Plains of Abraham at Quebec, died near Fredericton, New Brunswick, on 18 October 1819. [CG.3.11.1819]

SMELLIE, ANDREW, son of Richard Smellie in Glasgow, died in Kingston, Jamaica, in 1804. [SM.66.726]

SMITH, ANDREW, of the Glasgow Canadian Emigration Society, with his wife and family, emigrated via Greenock aboard the George Canning, Captain Potter, bound for Quebec on 14 April 1821. [TNA.CO42.189]

SMITH, ARCHIBALD, born 1794, from Glasgow, died in Madeira on 6 January 1823. [ARM]

SMITH, CUNNINGHAM, born 1813, son of William Smith of Carbeth-Guthrie and his wife Jane Cunningham, was educated at the University of Glasgow in 1827, a merchant in Glasgow and later in New York until 1850, died in Helensburgh, Dunbartonshire, on 21 February 1890. [ANY]

SMITH, ELIZABETH, daughter of John Smith a bookseller in Glasgow, married Francis Brown from Trinidad, in Glasgow on 11 October 1822. [BM.12.691]

SMITH, FARQUHAR, a labourer in Barrowfield, Glasgow, with Margaret his wife and two children, were bound for Canada in 1815. [TNA.CO385.2]

SMITH, JAMES, son of George Smith a cotton manufacturer in Glasgow, died in Nunce or Munee, St David, Jamaica, on 14 September 1804. [SM.66.973] [AJ.2970]

SMITH, JAMES, of the Strathaven and Kilbride Emigration Society, emigrated via Greenock aboard the George Canning, Captain Potter, bound for Quebec on 14 April 1821. [TNA.CO42.189]

SMITH, JAMES, of the Rutherglen Emigration Society, with his wife, three sons, and a daughter, emigrated via Greenock aboard the Commerce of Greenock, Captain Covendale, bound for Quebec on 11 May 1821. [TNA.CO42.189] [PAO]

SMITH, Reverend JAMES, late of the Secession Church in Nicolson Place, Lauriston, Glasgow, also of Washington, Pennsylvania, died at 13 Surrey Street, Lauriston, Glasgow, on 12 March 1845. [W.553]

SMITH, JOHN GUTHRIE, from Glasgow, fourth son of William Smith of Carbeth-Guthrie, married Anne Penelope Campbell Dennistoun, daughter of James Robert Dennistoun, in the British Embassy in Stuttgart, Germany, on 26 January 1861. [W.XXII.2272]

SMITH, Dr JOHN LEITCH, from Glasgow, died of cholera in Montreal, Quebec, on 17 June 1832. [AR.14.7.1832]

SMITH, NEIL, a surgeon from Glasgow, died at the Benin River, West Africa, on 11 June 1838. [SG.703]

SMITH, ROBERT, a gabbartman in Port Glasgow, in 1791. [NRS.S/H]

SMITH, ROBERT, in Kingston, Jamaica, co-owner of the Nancy of Glasgow in 1805. [NRS.CE60.11.8/63]

SMITH, ROBERT, a planter in New Montbleau, Jamaica, later in Glasgow, testament, 1821. [NRS.CC9.7.81.243]

SMITH, THOMAS, a labourer in Barrowfield, Glasgow, bound for Canada in 1815. [TNA.CO385.2]

SMITH, THOMAS, in Glasgow, a letter, 25 July 1839. [NRS.RD29.3.23]

SMITH, WILLIAM, of the Abercrombie Emigration Society, emigrated via Greenock aboard the David of London, master David Gemmil, bound for Quebec on 19 May 1821. [TNA.CO42.189]

SNEDDON, JAMES, of the Rutherglen Emigration Society, with his wife, son and daughter, emigrated via Greenock aboard the Commerce of Greenock, Captain Covendale, bound for Quebec on 11 May 1821, was granted land in Ramsay, Upper Canada, on 9 September 1821. [TNA.CO42.189] [PAO]

SNELL, Captain, master of the Portland of Glasgow from Leith with passengers bound for Van Diemen's Land, [Tasmania]. Australia, and New South Wales, on 1 April 1824, arrived in Hobart, Tasmania, on 10 September 1824. [LCL.XI.1156]; from Leith on 27 April 1826 with passengers bound for Australia, landed in Hobart on 14 August 1826, and in Sydney on 11 September 1826. [Hobart Town Gazette, 19.8.1826]

SOMERVILLE, DAVID, minister in Strathaven from 1766 to 1790, emigrated to USA, died in Rockbridge County, Virginia in June 1793. [UPC.2.225]; testament, 1799, Comm. Edinburgh. [NRS]

SOMERVILLE, JOHN, eldest son of Neil Somerville in Glasgow, died in Grenada on 20 October 1801. [SM.64.182]

SOMERVILLE, JOHN, in Glasgow, applied to settle in Canada on 26 February 1815. [NRS.RH9]

SOMERVILLE, JOHN, born 1815, a moulder in 74 Abercrombie Street, Glasgow, and his wife Ann born 1818, were bound for Australia in 1848. [BPP.11.164]

SOMMERVILLE, MARY, relict of Reverend William Horne in Braehead, died in Yorktown, Delaware County, Indiana, on 15 April 1850. [W.XI.1110]

SOMERVILLE, WILLIAM H., born 1794 in Glasgow, a butcher, emigrated via Liverpool to America, was naturalised in New York on 30 September 1819. [NY Court of Common Pleas]

SOMERVILLE, ANDREW BUCHANAN, of the Camlachie Emigration Society, with his two sons, emigrated via Greenock on board the Commerce of Greenock, Captain Coverdale, bound for Quebec on 11 May 1821, was granted land in Lanark, Upper Canada, on 28 July 1821. [TNA.CO42.89] [PAO]

SOMERVILLE, WILLIAM, born 1765, died 1 September 1837. [Ramshorn gravestone]

SOMERVILLE, WILLIAM, a partner in the company Ferguson and Company, cotton spinners and power loom cloth manufacturers in Glasgow, a bankrupt in 1848. [NRS.CS280.34.68]

SPENCER, THOMAS, second son of John Spencer a merchant in Jamaica, matriculated at Glasgow University in 1793. [MAGU]

STARK, JOHN, of the Hamilton Emigration Society, emigrated via Greenock on board the Commerce of Greenock, Captain Coverdale, bound for Quebec on 11 May 1821, was granted land in Dalhousie, Upper Canada, on 16 July 1821. [TNA.CO42.89] [PAO]

STARK, ROBERT, born 1828, a farrier in High Street, Glasgow, was accused of mobbing, rioting, theft, robbery and assault in 1850. [NRS.AD14.50.67]

STARK, SARAH, wife of John Craig an architect in Glasgow, died in Barcelona, Spain, when bound for Italy on 19 December 1792. [SM.55.50]

STARK, THOMAS, agent for the Bank of Scotland in Airdrie, 1849. [POD]

STEDMAN, Dr WILLIAM, born 13 June 1764, son of Thomas Steedman and his wife Ann Murray in Anderston, was educated at Glasgow University in 1782, a physician in St Croix, Danish West Indies, married Elizabeth Gordon, daughter of Dr George Gordon of St Kitts, in Glasgow on 2 February 1795; died in St Croix on 7 April 1844. [SM.57.132] [MAGU]

STEEL, ALEXANDER, of the Camlachie Emigration Society, with his wife, and four sons, emigrated via Greenock on board the Commerce of Greenock, Captain Coverdale, bound for Quebec on 11 May 1821, was granted land in Ramsay, Upper Canada, on 14 August 1821. [TNA.CO42.89] [PAO]

STEEL, GEORGE, of the Bridgeton Canadian Emigration Society, with his wife and family, emigrated via Greenock aboard the George Canning, Captain Potter, bound for Quebec on 14 April 1821. [TNA.CO42.189]

STEEL, ROBERT, son of Robert Steel a writer in Lanark, died in Chatham Estate, St James, Jamaica, on 17 March 1807. [SM.69.957]

STEEL, ROBERT, in Port Glasgow, a deed, 10 December 1841. [NRS.RD29.3.23]

STEEL, THOMAS, son of Robert Steel a writer in Lanark, died in Tobago in 1801. [AJ.2807]

STEEL, WILLIAM, son of Robert Steel a writer in Lanark and his wife Jean Ayton, [1769-1815], died in the West Indies. [Lanark gravestone]

STENHOUSE, JOHN, born 1830, son of Andrew Stenhouse and his wife Catherine Russell, died in New Zealand in 1876. [Maryhill gravestone]

STEPHENSON, DAVID, fifth son of Andrew Stephenson in Glasgow, died in Valparaiso, Chile, during an earthquake on 19 November 1822. [S.167.456]

STEVEN, JOHN, in New Providence, Bahamas, son and heir of James Steven a merchant tailor in Glasgow, 1803. [NRS.S/H]

STEVEN, WILLIAM, in St John, New Brunswick, brother and her of James Steven in Glasgow, who died 25 May 1853. [NRS.S/H]

STEVENSON, ALLAN, master of the Cherub of Glasgow from Greenock to Montreal, Quebec, in 1817 and 1818. [NRS.E504.15.115/119]

STEVENSON, GEORGE, of the Glasgow Wrights Emigration Society, with his wife, emigrated via Greenock aboard the George Canning, Captain Potter, bound for Quebec on 14 April 1821. [TNA.CO42.189]

STEVENSON, ROBERT, son of Allan Stevenson a wright in Glasgow, was apprenticed to Francis Innes, a gunsmith in Edinburgh, for seven years, on 17 August 1786. [ERA]

STEVENSON, THOMAS, first son of Thomas Stevenson in Jamaica, matriculated at Glasgow University in 1821. [MAGU]

STEWART, ALEXANDER, from Glasgow, a partner of the merchant company Thornton, Orr, and Company, in Grenada, was killed by Spanish privateers in January 1798 when on board the sloop George bound from Demerara to Martinique. [GC.1062] [AJ.2626]

STEWART, ALEXANDER, a skipper in Port Glasgow, testament, 1818, Comm. Glasgow. [NRS]

STEWART, ALEXANDER, of the Abercrombie Emigration Society, with his wife and family, emigrated via Greenock aboard the George Canning, Captain Potter, bound for Quebec on 14 April 1821. [TNA.CO42.189]

STEWART, ALEXANDER, of the Abercrombie Emigration Society, emigrated via Greenock aboard the George Canning, Captain Potter, bound for Quebec on 14 April 1821. [TNA.CO42.189]

STEWART, ARCHIBALD, of the Abercrombie Emigration Society, with his wife and family, emigrated via Greenock aboard the George Canning, Captain Potter, bound for Quebec on 14 April 1821. [TNA.CO42.189]

STEWART, DAVID, of the Glasgow Canadian Emigration Society, with his wife, emigrated via Greenock aboard the George Canning, Captain Potter, bound for Quebec on 14 April 1821. [TNA.CO42.189]

STEWART, HUGH, in St Croix, Danish Virgin Islands, died in Glasgow on 26 October 1826. [AJ.4115]

STEWART, JAMES, of the Bridgeton Transatlantic Emigration Society, emigrated via Greenock aboard the George Canning, Captain Potter, bound for Quebec on 14 April 1821. [TNA.CO42.189]

STEWART, JAMES, a merchant in Mexico later in Wellhall, Hamilton, dead by 1851, father of Helen, Nancy, Isett, Stewart in St Andrews, Fife, also of Octavius Stewart, and Patrick Stewart in Mexico, and James Hinton Stewart, and William Stewart, also Charles Haggart Stewart in Melbourne, Victoria, Australia. [NRS.S/H]

STEWART, JANET, daughter of James Stewart a vintner in Glasgow, married Thomas Walker, in Philadelphia, Pennsylvania, on 24 May 1838. [SG.675]

STEWART, JOHN, born 1806 in Glasgow, was educated at Glasgow University, minister of East Chapel of Hamilton from 1845 until 1851, died in 1853. [F.3.221]

STEWART, JOHN, of the Abercrombie Emigration Society, with his wife and family, emigrated via Greenock aboard the George Canning, Captain Potter, bound for Quebec on 14 April 1821. [TNA.CO42.189]

STEWART, JOHN, a carpenter in Blantyre, 1866, brother of William Stewart a clerk in New York who died in November 1848. [NRS.S/H]

STEWART, MARTIN, born 1826, a carter in Glasgow, Glasgow, was accused of mobbing, rioting, theft, robbery and assault in 1850. [NRS.AD14.50.67]

STEWART, PETER, a farmer in Balmore, with his wife Christian and five children, applied to emigrate to Canada in 1815. [TNA.CO385.2]

STEWART, ROBERT, a merchant, a partner in Dickson and Stewart, spirit dealers in Gallowgate, Glasgow, was admitted as a burgess and guilds-brother of Glasgow on 29 August 1810, as eldest son of John Stewart a gardener, burgess and guilds-brother. [GBR]

STEWART, WILLIAM, born 1800 in Lanarkshire, emigrated to America, a dry-goods broker in New York, died there on 18 November 1847. [ANY]

STEWART, WILLIAM A. D., from Glasgow, settled in St John's, New Brunswick, deeds, 1862, 1877. [NRS.RD5.1618.471; RD5.1634.142; RD5.1642.187]

STIRLING, CHARLES, a merchant in Glasgow, was appointed executor and factor of his brother Archibald Stirling in Hampden, Jamaica, sons of William Stirling of Keir, on 4 November 1793. [NRS.RD3.263.51]

STIRLING, Captain J., born 1792 in Lanarkshire, Lieutenant Governor of the Swan River Colony, Australia, in 1830. [BPP.3.436]

STIRLING, JOHN, a surgeon in Glasgow, and his wife Helen Rose, parents of Michael Finlayson Stirling a merchant in Belize, Honduras, in 1853. [NRS.S/H]

STIRLING, ROBERT, a merchant in Jamaica, co-owner of the Jane of Glasgow in 1806. [NRS.CE60.11.8/1]

STIRLING, WALTER, of the Bridgeton Transatlantic Emigration Society, with his wife and family, emigrated via Greenock aboard the George Canning, Captain Potter, bound for Quebec on 14 April 1821. [TNA.CO42.189]

STIRLING, WILLIAM, of the Bridgeton Canadian Emigration Society, with his wife and family, emigrated via Greenock aboard the George Canning, Captain Potter, bound for Quebec on 14 April 1821. [TNA.CO42.189]

STIRRAT, JAMES, was impressed into the Royal Navy in Nova Scotia in 1802, later with a wife and family in Cambuslang, Lanarkshire, applied to settle in Canada on 16 December 1819. [TNA.CO384.5.907]

STODART, ADAM, born 1783, died in New York on 27 July 1872. [Covington gravestone][S.9066]

STODART, MARION, born 1791, died in Louisville, Kentucky, on 9 July 1848. [Covington gravestone]

STORRY, ANDREW, third son of Andrew Storry a farmer in Shotts, Lanarkshire, educated at Glasgow University around 1780, a merchant in New York, died on 20 January 1820 in Kingston, New York. [ANY]

STORRIE, BARNELL, and son, from Blantyre, emigrated via Greenock aboard the Portaferry, bound for Quebec in May 1832. [QM.13.6.1832] [GWS]

STRACHAN, JOHN, born 1 December 1784, fourth son of Reverend William Strachan and his wife Elizabeth Howison in Culter, Biggar, a surgeon who died in Barbados on 30 September 1807. [SM.68.398] [F.1.247]

STRACHAN, THOMAS, of the Camlachie Emigration Society, with his wife, two sons, and three daughters, emigrated via Greenock on board the Commerce of Greenock, Captain Coverdale, bound for Quebec on 11 May 1821, was granted land in Lanark, Upper Canada, on 1 August 1821. [TNA.CO42.89] [PAO]

STRANG, Dr CHRISTOPHER, born 1849, died in Tarkisted, South Africa, on 28 August 1880. [East Kilbride gravestone]

STRANG, JOHN, son of John Strang in East Kilbride, a merchant who died in St Andrews, New Brunswick, on 1 August 1824. [BM.16.616][EA]

STRANGE, ISABELLA, wife of Archibald Campbell Hyndman in Lesmahagow, dead by 1859, aunt of Maxwell William Hyndman in Upper Canada. [NRS.S/H]

STRANGE, JAMES, from Glasgow, a merchant in Peterburg, Virginia, died on 15 June 1809. [SM.69.558]

STRANGE, JOHN MAXWELL, son of James M. Strange in Toronto, Ontario, heir to his grand-aunt Barbara Strange, wife of William Marshall a surgeon in Cambuslang, Lanarkshire, 1859. [NRS.S/H]

STRANGE, MAXWELL WILLIAM, in Upper Canada, nephew and heir of Isabella Strange, wife of Archibald Campbell Hyndman in Lesmahagow, Lanarkshire, 1859. [NRS.S/H]

STRATHEARN, JOHN, a journeyman wright from Kilmarnock, now in Glasgow, versus his wife Flora MacDougal, a servant in Broomhill, Lanark, a Process of Divorce in 1801. [NRS.CC8.6.1108]

STRUTHERS, ALEXANDER, a maltman, was admitted as a burgess and guilds-brother of Glasgow on 18 September 1794, as younger son of John Struthers, a maltman burgess and guilds-brother. [GBR]

STRUTHERS, ANDREW, in Canada West, son and heir of Alexander Struthers a cotton waste dealer in Glasgow, 1852. [NRS.S/H]

STRUTHERS, GAVIN, a Corporal of the 42nd Regiment, the Black Watch, son and heir of Alexander Struthers a weaver in Strathaven, Lanarkshire, who died 1 January 1851. [NRS.S/H]

STRUTHERS, JOHN, born in January 1764 in Glasgow, son of John Struthers, a maltman burgess, and his wife Hanna Stiven, a brewer who died aboard ship in the Savanna River, Georgia, on 24 February 1790. [Colonial Cemetery, Savanna, gravestone] [SM.52.205]

STRUTHERS, ROBERT, of the Strathaven and Kilbride Emigration Society, emigrated via Greenock aboard the George Canning, Captain Potter, bound for Quebec on 14 April 1821. [TNA.CO42.189]

STRUTHERS, WILLIAM, and family, from Bothwell, emigrated via Greenock aboard the Portaferry, bound for Quebec in May 1832. [QM.13.6.1832] [GWS]

STUART, DAVID KNOX, a physician in New Orleans, Louisiana, son of John Stuart of East Kilbride, died in New Orleans on 10 April 1851, [W.CII.1248]; testament, 1853. [NRS.SC70.1.81]

STUART, JOHN, from Glasgow, emigrated to Virginia before 1814. [OD]

STUART, JOHN, a merchant in Kingston, Jamaica, later in Glasgow by 1852. [NRS.CS313.858]; possibly died at 9 Roseberry Terrace, Glasgow, on 2 March 1877. [EC.28838]

STUART, JOHN, born 16 July 1822, educated at the Ratisbon Seminary in Germany in 1838, a Roman Catholic missionary, died in Glasgow on 12 January 1875. [SIG.295][RSC.I.256]

STUART, J., master of the Mount Stuart Elphinstone of Glasgow from Loch Boisdale with passengers bound for Quebec in 1849. [QM.30.8.1849]

STUART, WILLIAM MILLER, MD, son of John Stuart a tobacconist in Glasgow, died in Kingston, Jamaica, on 6 May 1832. [AJ.4408]

STUART, WILLIAM, born 1800 in Glasgow, died in Jamaica on 6 May 1835. [Scots Cemetery gravestone, Kingston, Jamaica]

SUMMERS, WILLIAM THOMAS, in Virginia, heir to his great great grandfather James Shaw a horse-letter in Port Glasgow, 1836. [NRS.S/H]

SUTHERLAND, ANN, born 1780, died in Toronto, Ontario, on 17 April 1847. [Lanark gravestone]

SUTHERLAND, DAVID, of the Glasgow Canadian Emigration Society, emigrated via Greenock aboard the George Canning, Captain Potter, bound for Quebec on 14 April 1821. [TNA.CO42.189]

SUTHERLAND, GEORGE, of the Glasgow Canadian Emigration Society, with his wife and family, emigrated via Greenock aboard the George Canning, Captain Potter, bound for Quebec on 14 April 1821. [TNA.CO42.189]

SWAN, ROBERT, in Coatbridge, a petition for sequestration in 1847. [NRS.CS279.2282]

SWAN, ROBERT, born 1802, son of John Swan and his wife Janet Williamson, died in America on 11 July 1878. [Carmichael grave]

SWORD, ARCHIBALD EWING, a merchant of the firm Sword, Muter and Company, manufacturers in Ingram Street, Glasgow, was admitted as a burgess and guilds-brother of Glasgow, as younger son of Alexander Sword a merchant burgess and guilds-brother on 5 July 1823. [GBR]

SYM, JAMES, a mathematical and optical instrument maker, was admitted as a burgess and guilds-brother of Glasgow on 26 July 1792, having served an apprenticeship with John Gardner, maltman and mathematical instrument maker, burgess and guilds-brother of Glasgow. [GBR]

SYME, Reverend ANDREW, from Lanarkshire, a tutor in Virginia, later ordained as a minister in 1791, minister at South Farnham, Va., from 1791 until 1794, then at Bristol, Dinwiddie County, Va., from 1794 to 1839. [OD]

SYMINGTON, THOMAS, born 1787 in Lanarkshire, managing director of the Shedden Company, died in Montreal, Quebec, on 6 August 1879. [EEC.29611]

TAIT, GEORGE, son of James Tait, an Exciseman in Glasgow, died on Sullivan's Island, near Charleston, South Carolina, on 30 August 1801. [GM.71.1053]

TAIT, SAMUEL, in Tradeston, applied to settle in Canada on 12 April 1827. [TNA.CO384.5.1049]

TASKER, WILLIAM, in Rotterdam, Zealand, was admitted as an honorary burgess and guilds-brother of Glasgow on 18 August 1790. [GBR]

TASSIE, J., agent for the Wester Bank in Strathaven in 1849. [POD]

TAYLOR, Mrs ANN, born 1773, from Hamilton, Lanarkshire, widow of William Taylor the Adjutant of the 27th Regiment, died in St John, New Brunswick, on 7 November 1832. [NBC.10.11.1832]

TAYLOR, ANN HELEN, second daughter of Alexander Taylor in Glasgow, married James Paterson, Monklands, St Thomas in the East, Jamaica, in St Andrew's church, Jamaica, on 8 January 1846. [AJ.5122]

TAYLOR, CHARLES JOHNSTONE, fourth son of Robert Taylor formerly a merchant in Jamaica, matriculated at Glasgow University in 1842. [MAGU]

TAYLOR, JAMES, born 1755 in Port Glasgow, emigrated to New York before 1776, a Loyalist who settled in New Brunswick in 1783, died in St John, N.B., on 26 December 1834. [NBRG.31.12.1834]

TAYLOR, JAMES, born 1769, a labourer and dyer from Carnwath, Lanarkshire, with Margaret Cowie his wife, Jean born 1796, Margaret born 1798, William born 1804, Mary born 1806, and Helen born 1808, applied to emigrate to Canada in 1815, emigrated via Greenock to Upper Canada in July 1815. [TNA.CO385.2; AO3]

TAYLOR, JANET, born 1794 in Port Glasgow, wife of Edward Taylor, died in St John, New Brunswick, on 6 May 1831. [NBC.7.5.1831]

TAYLOR, JOHN, a merchant in Jamaica, married Mary McCall, daughter of George McCall a merchant in Glasgow, there on 25 June 1793. [SM.55.307]

TAYLOR, JOHN, of Ballochneck, Stirlingshire, eldest son of Reverend Dr William Taylor, St Enoch's, Glasgow, died in Bardowie, St Andrew's, Jamaica, on 17 August 1829. [S.1029]

TAYLOR, Mrs MARGARET, wife of John Taylor a merchant in New York, and daughter of James Scott a merchant in Glasgow, died on 19 November 1797. [AJ.2609]

TAYLOR, PETER, of the Glasgow Trongate Emigration Society, emigrated via Greenock aboard the David of London, master David Gemmil, bound for Quebec on 19 May 1822. [TNA.CO42.189]

TAYLOR, R., master of the Susan of Glasgow from Glasgow with passengers bound for New York in 1849, also, with passengers bound for Quebec in 1851. [NARA][QM][BPP]

TAYLOR, WILLIAM, born 2 December 1790 in Glasgow, son of Reverend William Taylor, he was a Lieutenant General in the Service of the East India Company, died in New Zealand on 27 June 1868. [F.3.441]

TEASDALE, JOHN, from Larkhall, settled in Philadelphia, Pennsylvania, before 1848. [NRS.RH1.2.764]

TELFER, JEAN, widow of David Somerville minister of Strathaven, died in Lexington, Virginia, on 6 June 1800. [Glasgow Courier.1407] [Edinburgh Weekly Journal, 3/139]

TENNANT, ROBERT, born 1787 in Glasgow, a shop-keeper in Charleston, South Carolina, was naturalised there on 15 October 1813. [NARA.M1183.1]

THOM, ANDREW, a hammerman and saddletree maker of 32 Dunlop Street, Glasgow, was admitted as a burgess and guilds-brother of Glasgow, as married to Jeanie Douglas Muir, daughter of David Muir a hammerman, burgess and guilds-brother of Glasgow, on 19 August 1842. [GBR]

THOM, JOHN, born 1800, third son of John Thom a merchant in Glasgow, a land surveyor who died at Middleton College, Clarendon, Jamaica, on 15 April 1851, brother of Robert Thom the British Consul in Ningpo, China. [W.1224][AJ.5396]

THOM, ROBERT, a baker from Lanark, was naturalised in Charleston, South Carolina, in 1798. [NARA.M1183.1]

THOMAS, JANET, wife of James Torrie in Shawfield Bank, Rutherglen, Lanarkshire, dead by 1849, sister and heir of John Thomas in America. [NRS.S/H]

THOMAS, JOHN, second son of George Thomas a surgeon in Jamaica, matriculated at Glasgow University in 1813. [MAGU]

THOMSON, ANDREW, from Strathaven, Lanarkshire, was naturalised in New York on 31 December 1803. [NARA]

THOMSON, ARCHIBALD, from Hillhead, Glasgow, died in Hillhead, Jamaica, on 9 March 1821. [S.227.168][NRS.CS42.27.47]

THOMSON, ARCHIBALD, of the Hamilton Emigration Society, wit his wife and two sons, emigrated via Greenock on board the Commerce of Greenock, Captain Coverdale, bound for Quebec on 11 May 1821, was granted land in Dalhousie, Upper Canada, on 20 June 1821. [TNA.CO42.89] [PAO]

THOMSON, CATHERINE, daughter of John Thomson in Jamaica, married John Wilson, MD, from St Martin's, Dutch West Indies, in Glasgow on 7 November 1798. [GC.1122]

THOMSON, DANIEL, a tailor in Merion, Pennsylvania, heir of James Davidson a weaver in Glasgow, 1803. [NRS.S/H]

THOMSON, GEORGE, from Lanarkshire, settled in Charleston, South Carolina, probate 22 June 1796, S.C.

THOMSON, GEORGE, and wife, from Blantyre, emigrated via Greenock aboard the Portaferry, bound for Quebec in May 1832. [QM.13.6.1832] [GWS]

THOMSON, JAMES, born 1737, a pottery merchant in Turreen Street, Gallowgate, Glasgow, died in Glasgow on 30 August 1822. [SM.90.631]

THOMSON, JAMES, a gardener from Hamilton, a member of the Scots Charitable Society of Boston, Massachusetts, in 1767, there in 1787. [SCS/NEHGS]

THOMSON, JAMES, from Glasgow, a merchant in New York, died on 14 April 1820. [S.225.150][AJ.3826]

THOMSON, JAMES, in Kilbank, and his wife Ann Scott, [1783-1815], parents of James Thomson, born 1804, died 1836 in Quebec, and of Robert Thomson, born 1814, died 1840 in New York. [Lesmahagow gravestone]

THOMSON, JAMES, son of John Thomson in Glenim, died in September 1799, and his wife Mary Brown, died 1807, died in Jamaica. [Crawfordjohn gravestone]

THOMSON, JAMES, born 1807, late of Monteith Row, for fifty years a tea merchant at 263 Gallowgate, Glasgow, died at the residence of his son in Bridgewater-on-Laddon, Victoria, Australia, in 1884. [S.12856]

THOMSON, JAMES, in Bridgeton, Glasgow, applied to settle in Canada on 9 July 1819. [TNA.CO384.5.907]

THOMSON, Mrs JANET, died in Lanarkshire on 23 November 1825, mother of Reverend Martin in Halifax, Nova Scotia. [Acadian Recorder, 11.2.1826]

THOMSON, JOHN WEIR, youngest son of William Thomson and his wife Rachel Weir in Birkenhead, Lesmahagow, died in Hillside, St David, Jamaica on 29 July 1823. [Lesmahagow gravestone] [EA.6453.622]

THOMSON, JOHN, son of John Thomson in Glenim, died in September 1799, and his wife Mary Brown, died 1807, died in Jamaica. [Crawfordjohn gravestone]

THOMSON, JOHN, in Glasgow, late in St John's, Newfoundland, ca.1839. [RGNA.23.4.1839]

THOMSON, Reverend JOHN, married Elizabeth Cunningham, daughter of James Cunningham of Jocley's Barn, Jamaica, in Hamilton on 18 September 1845. [W.609]

THOMSON, JOHN, messenger at arms, Hamilton, 1849. [POD]

THOMSON, RALPH WARDLAW, in Bellary in the East Indies, son of Janet Crawford Wardlaw or Thomson there formerly in Garthamlock, Glasgow, 1854. [NRS.S/H]

THOMSON, ROBERT, born 1814 in Kilbank, son of J. Thomson and his wife Ann Scott, born 1763, died 1815, died in New York in 1840. [Lesmahagow gravestone]

THOMSON, ROBERT, in Clydebank, New South Wales, Australia, 1851, brother of James Thomson in Lauriston, Glasgow. [NRS.S/H]

THOMSON, SAMUEL, from Blantyre, emigrated via Greenock aboard the Portaferry, bound for Quebec in May 1832. [QM.13.6.1832] [GWS]

THOMSON, THOMAS, an attorney in Jamaica, eldest son of John Thomson in Glasgow, died in Bermuda on 14 February 1803. [EA.4115.03] [AJ.2692]

THOMSON, Dr THOMAS, Professor of Chemistry in Glasgow, father of Thomas Thomson a physician in Calcutta, India, in 1859. [NRS.S/H]

THOMSON, WILLIAM, in Glasgow, a deed, 5 July 1841. [NRS.RD29.3.23]

THORBURN, JOHN, born 1777, son of David Thorburn, [1742-1826], a tenant farmer in Roadhead, Quothquan, died on 5 March 1866 and was buried in Mount Royal Cemetery in Montreal, Quebec. [Carnwath gravestone]

THORBURN, WILLIAM, and Sons, versus Sir Alexander MacDonald Lockhart of Lee and Carnwath in 1814. [NRS.CS40.17.29]

TINNING, or BAIRD, ANN, was found guilty of theft and was sentenced in Glasgow in 1816, to 14 years transportation to the colonies. [NRS.GD1.959]

TOD, ..., born 1781, a merchant from Glasgow, with his sister born 1781, emigrated aboard the Draper bound for New York on 6 June 1801. [TNA.HO102.18]

TOMLINSON, JONATHAN, of the Camlachie Emigration Society, with his wife, three sons, and four daughters, emigrated via Greenock on board the Commerce of Greenock, Captain Coverdale, bound for Quebec on 11 May 1821, was granted land in Ramsay, Upper Canada, on 1 August 1821. [TNA.CO42.89] [PAO]

TOPPING, J., master of the Hope of Glasgow from Glasgow with passengers bound for Sydney, New South Wales, Australia, in July 1853, landed there on 23 November 1853. [LCL.4226/4275]

TORRANCE, MARY, youngest daughter of John Torrance a manufacturer in Stonehouse, married David Dickie a teacher in USA on 18 November 1839. [EEC.19978]

TOSHACK, JOHN, jr.,, of the Rutherglen Emigration Society, emigrated via Greenock aboard the Commerce of Greenock, Captain Covendale, bound for Quebec on 11 May 1821, was granted land in Upper Canada, on 9 September 1821. [TNA.CO42.189] [PAO]

TOSHACH, WILLIAM, of the Rutherglen Emigration Society, emigrated via Greenock aboard the Commerce of Greenock, Captain Covendale, bound for Quebec on 11 May 1821, was granted land in Ramsay, Upper Canada, on 9 September 1821. [TNA.CO42.189] [PAO]

TROKES, MAXWELL, born 1781, a merchant in Virginia, died in Glasgow on 4 December 1852, husband of Sarah H. Wood who died on 2 November 1857. [Blackfriars gravestone, Glasgow]

TROOP, Captain ANDREW, from Port Glasgow, and Elizabeth McKerley of Halifax, Nova Scotia, were married there on 4 February 1815. [AR.11.2.1815]

TULLY, JOHN, of the Hamilton Emigration Society, with his family, emigrated via Greenock on board the Commerce of Greenock, Captain Coverdale, bound for Quebec on 11 May 1821. [TNA.CO42.89]

TURNBULL, JAMES, master of the Flora of Port Glasgow landed in Sydney, New South Wales, Australia, on 1 November 1845 from

Glasgow with passengers bound for Port Philip and Sydney in 1849, [SG.18.1796]; with passengers bound for Australia in 1853. [LCL.4224]

TURNBULL, LAURENCE, master of the Sherbrook of Port Glasgow trading between Cork and Alloa in 1815. [NRS.E504.2.13]

TURNBULL, Dr LAURENCE, born 10 September 1821 in Shotts, Lanarkshire, emigrated to America in 1838, a pharmacist who died in Philadelphia, Pennsylvania, on 24 October 1900. [AP]

TURNBULL, ROBERT, from Cumbernauld, a divinity student in 1826, later a minister in Boston, Massachusetts. [AUPC]

TURNBULL, WILLIAM, a bookseller, died in Glasgow on 6 September 1822. [SM.90.632]

TURNER, ALLAN, son of Allan Turner, a calico printer in Glasgow, and his wife Margaret Turner, was apprenticed as a sailor to Captain Joseph Campbell master of the Jenny of Wiscafull of Lincoln County, Massachusetts, on 17 October 1793. [NRS.RD2.254.813]

TURNER, ARCHIBALD, a weaver, was admitted as a burgess and guildsbrother of Glasgow on 11 February 1792. [GBR]

TURNER, ARCHIBALD, son of Archibald Turner a weaver in Glasgow, a writer in Glasgow who was admitted as a Notary Public on 28 June 1799. [NRS.NP2.36.281]

TURNER, DOUGALD, in Australia, son and heir of Robert Turner, a weaver in Glasgow, in 1857. [NRS.S/H]

TURNER, ROBERT, a weaver in Glasgow, father of Dougald Turner in Australia, in 1859. [NRS.S/H]

TURNER, SUSAN, born 1824 in America, a piecer in Tontine Close, Glasgow, accused of theft in 1854. [NRS.AD14.54.138]

TURNER, Captain, master of the Lanarkshire of Glasgow from Glasgow with passengers bound for Quebec in 1849. [QM.23.6.1849]

TWEEDIE, JEAN, daughter of James Tweedie in Gateside of Coulter, versus William Thomson, nephew of Alexander Thomson tenant of Wolf Clyde, a clock and watchmaker in Biggar, 18 June 1792. [NRS.CC8.6.1900]

UMPHERSTON, ARCHIBALD, born 1820, an agricultural labourer from Tollcross, Glasgow, with his wife Janet born 1823, and three children, emigrated to South Australia in 1849. [BPP.11.198]

UMPHERSTON, WILLIAM, born 1830, from Cambuslang, Lanarkshire, emigrated to South Australia in 1848. [BPP.11.164]

URE, JANET, daughter of William Ure in Glasgow, married James Scott from Montreal, Quebec, on 12 April 1831. [FH.476]

URE, JOHN, from Glasgow, died at Aux Cayes, St Domingo, on 20 June 1820. [BM.7.705]

VEITCH, ANDREW, in Lanarkshire, graduated MD from King's College, Aberdeen, on 24 June 1809. [KCA]

VERE, ELIZABETH WEIR, relict of Houghton Bowman, died in Glasgow on 14 September 1822. [SM.90.632]

VERTUE, JAMES, a supercargo from Glasgow, when bound for New Providence in the Bahamas aboard the Tirselet, drowned in 1799. [NRS.CC9.7.77]

VIRTUE, JOHN, of the Lanarkshire Emigration Society, with family, emigrated to Canada on the Earl of Buckinghamshire, Captain Johnston, on 29 April 1821. [TNA.CO42.189]

VIRTUE, JOHN, of the Lanarkshire Emigration Society, emigrated to Canada on the Earl of Buckinghamshire, Captain Johnston, on 29 April 1821. [TNA.CO42.189]

WADDELL, GEORGE, a merchant from Glasgow, settled in North America before 1806. [NRS.CS17.1.25/329]

WADDELL, JAMES, of Leadloch, Auchtermuir, dead by 1854, father of James Waddell a merchant in Canada. [NRS.S/H]

WADDELL, JAMES, born 1825, from Stonefield, Glasgow, died 2 January 1850, was buried in the British Cemetery, Funchal, Madeira. [ARM]

WADDEL, JOHN, born 10 April 1771, son of James Waddel in Shotts, educated at Glasgow University from 1788 to 1793, a minister in Truro, Nova Scotia, from 1798, died on 13 November 1842. [MAGU][UPC]

WADDELL, or GILCHRIST, Mrs MARGARET, in Carluke, versus the Ballochmy Railway Company in 1847. [NRS.CS97.W.2.9]

WADDELL, Mrs, relict of Matthew Waddell in Jamaica, died in Lanark in 1817. [S.18]

WALKER, ANDREW, second son of Reverend James Walker in Carnwath, died in Bowmanville, Canada West, on 6 January 1856. [W.XVII.1731]

WALKER, JAMES WILSON, born 1823, a carter in Bridgeton, Glasgow, Glasgow, was accused of mobbing, rioting, theft, robbery and assault in 1850. [NRS.AD14.50.67]

WALKER, JOHN, from Glasgow, settled in Boston, Massachusetts, by 1803. [NRS.AC7.76]

WALKER, ROBERT, born 2 June 1795 in Govan, Glasgow, son of William Walker and his wife Janet, a boot and shoemaker, husband of Christian born 1795 in Glasgow, parents of Mary born 1818 in Glasgow, were naturalised on 19 March 1827. [New York Court of Common Pleas]

WALKER, WILLIAM, born 1788, second son of David Walker a manufacturer in the Gorbals, Glasgow, died on the Iter Boreale Estate, Jamaica, in June 1810. [EA.4885.255]

WALKINSHAW, ROBERT, of Parkhouse, born 1756, died 12 September 1835, husband of Jean Munro. [Ramshorn gravestone]

WALLACE, ANDREW, master of the Unity of Port Glasgow from Greenock to New Brunswick in 1816. [NRS.E504.15.100]

WALLACE, DAVID, master of the William of Glasgow from Greenock to New Orleans, Louisiana, in 1817; master of the Maria of Glasgow from Greenock to Halifax, Nova Scotia, in 1818. [NRS.E504.15.115/122]

WALLACE, HUGH RITCHIE, born in Glasgow, first son of Hugh Wallace formerly of Biscany, Jamaica, matriculated at Glasgow University in 1802. [MAGU]

WALLACE, HUGH, of the Glasgow Trongate Emigration Society, with his wife and family, emigrated via Greenock aboard the David of London, master David Gemmil, bound for Quebec on 19 May 1821. [TNA.CO42.189]

WALLACE, HUGH, a weaver from Glasgow, settled in Dalhousie township, Upper Canada, around 1821. [BPP.2.167]

WALLACE, JAMES, born 1789, son of Archibald Wallace a merchant in Glasgow, died in Jamaica on 23 January 1820. [Glasgow, Greyfriars, graveyard]

WALLACE, JOHN, born 6 November 1827 in Pollockshaws, Glasgow, son of John Wallace and his wife Agnes McGhee, was educated at Glasgow University, a minister at North Shore, New Zealand, from 1866 to 1880, died in Glenbuck on 3 December 1895. [F.3.44]

WALLACE, MARION, widow of John Galbreath in Glasgow, married Benjamin Heath, a physician from Jamaica, in Edinburgh on 3 November 1790. [EMR]

WARDEN, JAMES, from Glasgow, died in Paterson, New Jersey, in 1852. [S.29.1.1853]

WARDLAW, WILLIAM, jr., a merchant, partner of William Wardlaw and Company in Smith Court, Glasgow, was admitted as a burgess and guilds-brother of Glasgow, on 6 January 1818, as eldest son of Gilbert Wardlaw a merchant, burgess and guilds-brother. [GBR]

WARDROP, DANIEL, born 1765 in Glasgow, a merchant who emigrated to America, died in Virginia in 1791. [SRA]

WARK, ALEXANDER, President of the Rutherglen Emigration Society, with his wife, son and two daughters, emigrated via Greenock aboard the Commerce of Greenock, Captain Covendale, bound for Quebec on 11 May 1821, was granted land in Lanark, Upper Canada, on 22 August 1822. [TNA.CO42.189] [PAO]

WARNOCK, JAMES, born 1785, farmer at Bankhead, died 29 August 1860, husband of Jane Gilmour, born 1811, died on 12 November 1898. [Carmunnock gravestone]

WARNOCK, JOHN, of the Rutherglen Emigration Society, emigrated via Greenock aboard the Commerce of Greenock, Captain Covendale, bound for Quebec on 11 May 1821, was granted land in Sherbrook, Upper Canada, on 8 August 1821. [TNA.CO42.189] [PAO]

WATSON, ALEXANDER, from Glasgow, later in America, died at sea in July 1857, inventory, 1858, Edinburgh. [NRS]

WATSON, Dr GAVIN, born 20 June 1796 in Pettinain, son of John Watson and his wife Janet McCrocket, was educated at Glasgow University, a physician and surgeon, later a botanist, who emigrated to Philadelphia, Pennsylvania, in 1823, died there on 28 October 1858. [AP]

WATSON, GEORGE, born 1791, son of Thomas Watson in Glasgow, a student at Glasgow University in 1807, later a surgeon and lecturer in USA from 1818 until his death in New York on 12 November 1851. [MAGU]

WATSON, JANET, widow of James Thomson in Douglas, dead by 1857, sister of William Watson a wood-merchant in Canada East. [NRS.S/H]

WATSON, or SCOTT, JESSIE, in Hamburg, Germany, daughter and heir of Reverend John Walker of the Relief Church in Glasgow, 28 November 1835. [NRS.S/H]

WATSON, JOHN, son of Reverend Watson in Glasgow, died at Pint St Charles, near Montreal, Quebec, on 6 May 1820. [S.4.183][EA.5910]

WATSON, JOHN, in Glasgow, his mother's will, 22 October 1838. [NRS.RD29.3.23]

WATSON, JOHN COOPER, infant son of William Wilson a bookseller from Glasgow, died at sea off the Banks of Newfoundland on 2 July 1844. [SG.1324]

WATSON, MALCOLM, master of the Maria of Glasgow from Greenock to Miramachi, New Brunswick, in 1816. [NRS.E504.15.122]; master of the Unity of Port Glasgow from Greenock to Miramachi, N.B., in 1816. [NRS.E504.15.122]

WATSON, THOMAS, a surgeon, son of William Watson in Glasgow, died at Black River, Jamaica, in 1798. [SM.60.719] [AJ.2652]

WATSON, WILLIAM, a wood merchant in Canada East, brother and heir of Janet Watson, widow of James Thomson in Douglas, Lanarkshire, 1857. [NRS.S/H]

WATSON, WILLIAM, a butcher in Lafayette, New York, son and heir to Alexander Watson a clerk in the Clyde Ironworks, Glasgow, who died on 20 December 1865. [NRS.S/H]

WATT, JAMES, a merchant, son of James Watt a tobacconist in Glasgow, died on St Vincent in March 1801. [GC.1600]

WATT, JAMES, of the Glasgow Trongate Emigration Society, with his wife and child, emigrated via Greenock aboard the David of London, master David Gemmil, bound for Quebec on 19 May 1821. [TNA.CO42.189]

WATT, MARGARET, wife of Thomas Orsali in Montreal, Quebec, heir to her grandfather Thomas Watt a tailor in Cambusnethan, Lanarkshire, 1854. [NRS.S/H]

WATT, THOMAS, of the Glasgow Trongate Emigration Society, with emigrated via Greenock aboard the David of London, master David Gemmil, bound for Quebec on 19 May 1821. [TNA.CO42.189]

WATT, THOMAS, a tailor in Cambusnethan, Lanarkshire, dead by 1854. [NRS.S/H]

WATT, WILLIAM, born 1745, a mason, a resident of Tobago for 24 years, died in Brest, France, on 7 January 1795, husband of Jean Fisher born 1745, died 1819. [Symington gravestone]

WATT, WILLIAM, born 1770, son of John Watt [1738-1782], a mason in Symington, and his wife Jean Fisher, [1745-1819], died in Tobago in 1793. [Symington gravestone]

WEIR, ABRAHAM, a miner in Leadhills, father of James Weir a merchant in Fredericksburg, Virginia, a bond dated May 1785. [NRS.RD2.240/2.479]

WEIR, JOHN, born 1766, son of John Weir, [1723-1798], and his wife Jean Morton, [1735-1778], died in Jamaica in 1796. [Lesmahagow gravestone]

WEST, MAURICE, a merchant in Kingston, Jamaica, co-owner of Glasgow registered ships between 1793 and 1803. [NRS.CE60.11.3/65; 5/21; G.1.67/106; 8/27]

WHARRIE, HUGH, son of Robert Wharrie of Pathhead, a surgeon, [1748-1818], and his wife Elizabeth Smith, [1753-1825], died in Jamaica in 1809. [Lesmahagow gravestone].

WHARRIE, Dr PATRICK SMITH, son of Robert Wharrie of Pathhead, a surgeon, [1748-1818], and his wife Elizabeth Smith, [1753-1825], died in Nelson, Upper Canada, on 27 February 1844. [Lesmahagow gravestone].

WHARRY, THOMAS, in Hamilton, graduated MD from King's College, Aberdeen, on 31 January 1804. [KCA]

WHITE, ALEXANDER, of the Bridgeton Transatlantic Emigration Society, with his wife and family, emigrated via Greenock aboard the George Canning, Captain Potter, bound for Quebec on 14 April 1821. [TNA.CO42.189]

WHITE, ANDREW, in Glasgow, a deed, 29 October 1841. [NRS.RD29.3.23]

WHITE, WILLIAM, from Glasgow, died between Liverpool and Shelborne, Nova Scotia, on 9 December 1786. [NSGWC.2.1.1787]

WHITE, WILLIAM, of the Glasgow Wrights Emigration Society, with his wife, emigrated via Greenock aboard the George Canning, Captain Potter, bound for Quebec on 14 April 1821. [TNA.CO42.189]

WHITEFORD, JANE, in Lesmahagow, dead by 1852. [NRS.S/H]

WHITEFORD, JOHN, with ten dependents, members of the Lesmahagow Emigration Society of Lanark, emigrated to Quebec in 1820. [TNA.CO384.6.10.1062]

WHITEFORD, WILLIAM, in Montreal, Quebec, heir to his grandmother Jane Whiteford in Lesmahagow, Lanarkshire, 1852. [NRS.S/H]

WHITELAW, JAMES, born 1747, son of William Whitelaw in Whiteinch, Lanarkshire, a surveyor, from Greenock to Philadelphia, Pennsylvania, aboard the Matty on 24 May 1773, settled in Rygate, Vermont, died there in 1829. [TNA.T47.12][VHS]

WHYTLAW, JOHN, in Mississippi, heir to his uncle John Whytlaw, merchant from Glasgow settled on Bay Island, New Zealand, 1853. [NRS.S/H]

WIGAND, JOHN, possibly from Glasgow, a volunteer under Garibaldi in Italy in 1860. [SHR.57.176]

WILKIE, DANIEL, born 1777 in Bothwell, son of James Wilkie a farmer, was educated at Glasgow University from 1794 to 1803, emigrated to Quebec in 1804, a classics teacher, preacher and journalist in Montreal, died in 1851, buried in Mount Herman Cemetery. [MAGU]

WILKIE, DAVID, from Glasgow, settled in Jamaica, died 12 October 1808, testament, 13 April 1809, Comm. Edinburgh. [NRS]

WILKIE, JAMES, of the Cambuslang Emigration Society, with his wife and family, emigrated via Greenock aboard the George Canning, Captain Potter, bound for Quebec on 14 April 1821. [TNA.CO42.189]

WILKIE, THOMAS, a merchant in Glasgow, later in Kingston, Jamaica, died in 1794, testament, 22 November 1794, Comm. Edinburgh. [NRS]

WILKIE, WILLIAM, in Rantoles Ridge, South Carolina, son and heir of Peter Wilkie a grocer in Glasgow, 1832. [NRS.S/H]

WILLIAMS, ROBERT, son of Isabella Marshall or Williams in Glasgow, emigrated to Jamaica in 1819, settled on Sutton's Estate, Clarendon parish, Jamaica, died in 1823. [UNC; Williams pp]

WILSON, ALEXANDER, born 1740, a slater, died 11 March 1815, husband of Elizabet Dean, parents of Alexander Wilson, born 1777, a goldsmith, died 12 March 1808. [Ramshorn gravestone]

WILSON, FRANCIS, messenger at arms, Strathaven, 1849. [POD]

WILSON, JAMES, in St James, Cornwall County, Jamaica, appointed his brother William Wilson in Shotts as his attorney on 3 November 1814. [NRS.RD5.271.425]

WILSON, JAMES, of the Glasgow Trongate Emigration Society, with his wife and family, emigrated via Greenock aboard the David of London, master David Gemmil, bound for Quebec on 19 May 1821. [TNA.CO42.189]

WILSON, JANET, with three children, members of the Lesmahagow Emigration Society of Lanark, emigrated to Quebec in 1820. [TNA.CO384.6.101062]

WILSON, JOHN, born 1789 in Lanarkshire, an engineer and surveyor in Charleston, South Carolina, applied for naturalisation there on 7 May 1814. [NARA.M1183.1]

WILSON, JOHN, in Rutherglen, a blacksmith and army pensioner, with his wife and four children, applied to settle in Canada on 6 June 1827. [TNA.CO384.5.1073]

WILSON, JOHN RUSSELL, born 1809, a baker from Glasgow, eldest son of John Wilson a miller, died in Halifax, Nova Scotia, on 21 September 1873. [GH.10547]

WILSON, MARY, from Lanark, later in Alleghany City, Philadelphia, [sic], married Reverend William College of the Ligonier Valley, in Alleghany City on 3 March 1853. [EEC.22413]

WILSON, ROBERT, born 1847, son of John Wilson in 25 Napiershall Street, Glasgow, died in Philadelphia, Pennsylvania, on 19 January 1873. [EC.27568]; testament, 1873, Edinburgh S.C., [NRS]

WILSON, WILLIAM, a gentleman in Shotts, Lanarkshire, executor of his brother James Wilson in St James, Cornwall, Jamaica, 3 November 1814. [NRS.RD5.425]

WILSON, WILLIAM, in Glasgow, applied to settle in Canada on 26 February 1815. [NRS.RH9]

WILSON, WILLIAM, son of Adam Wilson in Glasgow, was educated at King's College, Aberdeen, from 1820 until 1823, a merchant in Jamaica and in New South Wales, Australia. [KCA]

WINGATE, LOUISA JANE, born 1822, from Glasgow, youngest daughter of Andrew Wingate, died in Madeira on 16 April 1844, was buried in the British Cemetery, Funchal, Madeira. [W.V.464][ARM]

WINNING, JOHN, of the Lesmahagow Emigration Society, emigrated to Canada on the Earl of Buckinghamshire, Captain Johnston, on 29 April 1821. [TNA.CO42.189]

WINNING, JOHN B., from New Lanark, was in Philadelphia, Pennsylvania, a letter, 1835. [NLS.Acc.6913]

WINNING, WILLIAM, born 1790 in Lanarkshire, a pocketbook maker, emigrated to New York, naturalised there on 29 May 1821. [NARA]

WODROP, WILLIAM, born 1745, died in Dumbreck, Glasgow, on 20 August 1822. [SM.90.520]

WOODS, ELIZA, daughter of John Woods in Glasgow, married Alfred Pell in New York on 17 February 1848. [SG.1699]

WOOD, GEORGE, born 1794 in Port Glasgow, a merchant who was naturalised in New York on 3 May 1817. [NY Court of Common Pleas]

WOOD, GEORGE, master of the Penelope of Glasgow from Greenock to Halifax, Nova Scotia, in 1813. [NRS.E504.15.99]

WOOD, JOHN, eldest son of Reverend Charles Wood in Wiston, died at Grange Estate, Jamaica, on 13 January 1819. [EA]

WOOD, WILLIAM, late in Jamaica, died in Port Glasgow on 24 October 1806. [GrA.31.10.1806] [NRS.RD Renfrew.8647; SC58.1.9]

WOOD, WILLIAM, in Green Street Lane, Bridgeton, Glasgow, applied to settle in Canada on 9 April 1827. [TNA.CO384.5.1065]

WOOD, WILLIAM, born 21 October 1808 in Glasgow, a banker in New York by 1828, died there on 1 October 1894. [ANY]

WORDIE, JAMES, third son of Thomas Wordie a craftsman in Denny, matriculated at Glasgow University in 1809, a minister in Kingston, Jamaica, from 1823 to 1843, later in Cupar, Fife, died on 3 August 1862. [F.7.671][MAGU]

WORTHINGTON, AGNES, a girl, was found guilty in Glasgow of stealing a watch, was sentenced to 7 years transportation to the colonies in 1815. [NRS.GD1.959]

WOTHERSPOON, ANDREW, a mason, was admitted as a burgess and guilds-brother of Glasgow on 28 June 1781, testament, 1791, Comm. Glasgow. [NRS][GBR]

WOTHERSPOON, ROBERT, a baker, was admitted as a burgess and guilds-brother of Glasgow on 18 May 1797, by right of his wife Jean Reid, daughter of Robert Reid a baker burgess and guildsbrother. [GBR]

WOTHERSPOON, ROBERT, born 1805 in Glasgow, a merchant in Charleston, South Carolina, who was naturalised there on 27 July 1831. [NARA.M1183.1]

WRIGHT, Captain, master of the Leven Lass of Glasgow from Glasgow with passengers bound for Quebec in 1842. [GCA.TCN.21/2]

WYLLIE, HUGH, a merchant in Williamsburgh, Granville County, North Carolina, eldest son of Hugh Wyllie, a merchant and former Lord Provost of Glasgow, appointed John Hay, a merchant in Glasgow, as his factor and attorney, on 11 February 1787. [NRS.RD2.242/1.757]

WYLLIE, JOHN, master of the Norval of Glasgow to North Carolina in 1792 and 1793. [GC.12.4.1792; 9.2.1793]

WYLLIE, J. master of the Jane Brown of Glasgow from Glasgow to Quebec in 1842, [GH.13.6.1842], also in 1843, Favourite of Port Glasgow from Glasgow with passengers to Quebec in 1848, 1849, also, as master of the Susan of Glasgow from Glasgow with passengers bound for Quebec in 1852. [GA]

WYSE, DAVID, a steamboat master in Glasgow who died on 17 March 1851, father of John Wyse a mariner in Australia, 1854. [NRS.S/H]

YOUNG, CHRISTIAN, was found guilty of theft, and was sentenced, in Glasgow, to 14 years transportation to the colonies in 1816. [NRS.GD1.959]

YOUNG, Miss EDMONSTONE, from Glasgow, died in Kingston, Jamaica, in 1817. [S.19]

YOUNG, HUGH, a farmer at Conderrat, Lanarkshire, testament, 1798, Comm. Glasgow. [NRS]

YOUNG, JAMES, of the Govan Emigration Society, with his wife, son, and seven daughters, emigrated via Greenock on board the Commerce of Greenock, Captain Coverdale, bound for Quebec on 11 May 1821, was granted land in Lanark, Upper Canada, on 26 July 1821. [TNA.CO42.89] [PAO]

YOUNG, JAMES, settled at Pimento Grove, St Dorothy's, Jamaica, son of John Young in Glasgow, died in Jamaica on 12 October 1838. [SG.8/745]

YOUNG, JOHN, son of William Young a merchant in Glasgow, died in Trelawney, Jamaica, on 26 December 1817. [AJ.3660] [S.I.29]

YOUNG, JOHN, President of the Abercrombie Emigration Society, with his wife, emigrated via Greenock aboard the David of London, master David Gemmil, bound for Quebec on 19 May 1821. [TNA.CO42.189]

YOUNG, JOHN, first son of John Young in Jamaica, matriculated at the University of Glasgow in 1833. [MAGU]

YOUNG, JOHN, from Glasgow, married Elisa Orsini, youngest daughter of Dr Alexander Orsini, Procurator at the Tuscan Law Courts, in Leghorn/Livorno, Italy, on 13 September 1854. [W.XV.1584]

YOUNG, LILLIAS M., daughter of James Young in Peelhill, married Charles Stott from Washington, D.C., in Philadelphia on 7 July 1846. [W.VII.703]

YOUNG, ROBERT, of the Camlachie Emigration Society, emigrated via Greenock on board the Commerce of Greenock, Captain Coverdale, bound for Quebec on 11 May 1821, was granted land in Lanark, Upper Canada, on 28 July 1821. [TNA.CO42.89] [PAO]

YOUNG, ROBERT, born 1792 in Glasgow, died in Madeira on 8 July 1825. [ARM]

YOUNG, WILLIAM, son of John Young in Kilsyth, emigrated via Greenock to Port Philip, Victoria, Australia, in 1848. [NRS.GD171.1327/2]

YOUNGER, GEORGE, a merchant was admitted as a burgess and guilds-brother of Glasgow on 2 August 1770, as eldest son of Andrew Younger a barber burgess and guilds-brother, testament, 1792, Comm. Glasgow. [NRS][GBR]

YOUNGER, THOMAS, born 16 August 1747, son of Andrew Younger and his wife Helen House, emigrated from Glasgow to Wilmington, North Carolina, died in Lucie, Jamaica, in 1795. [GM.65.794]

YOUNGER, THOMAS, born 16 August 1747, son of Andrew Younger and his wife Helen House, emigrated from Glasgow to Wilmington, North Carolina, died in Lucie, Jamaica, in 1795.

YUILL, JAMES, sr., President of the Abercrombie Emigration Society, with his wife and family, emigrated via Greenock aboard the George Canning, Captain Potter, bound for Quebec on 14 April 1821. [TNA.CO42.189]

YUILL, JOHN, jr, of the Abercrombie Emigration Society, with his wife, emigrated via Greenock aboard the George Canning, Captain Potter, bound for Quebec on 14 April 1821. [TNA.CO42.189]

YUILL, WILLIAM, a thread-maker in Glasgow, testament, 1793, Comm. Glasgow. [NRS]

REFERENCES

ABR Ayr Burgess Roll

AJ Aberdeen Journal, series

ANY St Andrews Society of New York

AO Annan Observer, series

AP St Andrews Society of Philadelphia

AR Acadian Recorder, series

ARM Madeira Regional Archives

AUPC Annals of the United Presbyterian Church

BA Officers of the Bengal Army, 1758-1834

BM Blackwood's Magazine, series

BPP British Parliamentary Papers, series

~~Car~~ Caribbeana, series

CG City Gazette, series

CM Caledonian Mercury, series

CMF History of Clan MacFarlane, [Glasgow, 1922]

CMSA Colonial Museum & Savanna Advertiser, series

DC Dundee Courier, series

DCB Dictionary of Canadian Biography

DGH Dumfries and Galloway Herald, series

DPCA Dundee, Perth, and Courier Advertiser, series

DU Duke University, North Carolina

EA Edinburgh Advertiser, series

EC Edinburgh Courant, series

EEC Edinburgh Evening Courant, series

EMR Edinburgh Marriage Register

ERA Edinburgh Register of Apprentices

F Fasti Ecclesiae Scoticanae

FH Fife Herald, series

GBR Glasgow Burgess Roll

GCA Glasgow City Archives

GCS Georgia for the Country, Savanna, series

GH Glasgow Herald, series

GkAd Greenock Advertiser, series

GM Gentleman's Magazine, series

GSP Glasgow Sunday Post, series

GUMA Glasgow University Matriculation Album

GWS Glasgow & West Scotland Family History Society

HBRS Hudson Bay Records Society

HCA History of the County of Ayr, [Edinburgh, 1852]

HHG History of Hutcheson's Hospital, [Glasgow, 1881]

HPC History of the Presbyterian Church

INC Immigrants to North Carolina

JRG Jamaica Royal Gazette, series

KCA King's College, Aberdeen

LCL Lloyd's Commercial Lists, series

MG McClellands in Galloway, [Edinburgh, 1996]

NARA National Archives, Records Administration

NBC New Brunswick Courier, series

NBRG New Brunswick Royal Gazette, series

NCSA North Carolina State Archives

NEHGS New England Historic Genealogical Society

NJA New Jersey Archives

NLS National Library of Scotland

NRS National Records of Scotland

NSRG Nova Scotia Royal Gazette, series

NSW New South Wales, passenger arrivals

OD Scots in the Old Dominion, [Edinburgh, 1980]

OPR Old Parish Register

PAO Public Archives of Ontario

PANB Public Archives of New Brunswick

PCC Prerogative Court of Canterbury

POD Post Office Directory

RGG Register of Glasgow Graduates

RGNA Royal Gazette of North America, series

RSC Records of the Scots Colleges

QCG Quebec City Gazette, series

QM Quebec Mercury, series

S Scotsman, series

SEC Scottish Episcopalian Clergy, 1680-2000

SG Scottish Guardian, series

SGS Scottish Genealogy Society

SHR Scottish Historical Review, series

SIG Scots in Germany, Edinburgh 1902

SM Scots Magazine, series

SOF Some Old Families, Birmingham 1890

SRA Strathclyde Regional Archives

TNA The National Archives of the UK

UNC University of North Carolina

UPC United Presbyterian Church

VHS Vermont Historical Society

VMHB Virginia Magazine of History and Biography, series

W Witness, series

WS History of the Society of Writers to the Signet

WSP Washington State Pioneers

www.ingramcontent.com/pod-product-compliance
Lightning Source LLC
Chambersburg PA
CBHW071847230426
43671CB00012B/2096